breaking
free
from myths about
teaching and learning

ASCD MEMBER BOOK

Many ASCD members received this book as a
member benefit upon its initial release.

Learn more at: **www.ascd.org/memberbooks**

breaking free

from myths about teaching and learning

innovation as an engine for student success

Allison Zmuda

Alexandria, Virginia USA

1703 N. Beauregard St. • Alexandria, VA 22311-1714 USA
Phone: 800-933-2723 or 703-578-9600 • Fax: 703-575-5400
Web site: www.ascd.org • E-mail: member@ascd.org
Author guidelines: www.ascd.org/write

Gene R. Carter, *Executive Director;* Judy Zimny, *Chief Program Development Officer;* Nancy Modrak, *Publisher;* Scott Willis, *Director, Book Acquisitions & Development;* Julie Houtz, *Director, Book Editing & Production;* Ernesto Yermoli, *Editor;* Catherine Guyer, *Senior Graphic Designer;* Mike Kalyan, *Production Manager;* Keith Demmons, *Desktop Publishing Specialist*

ASCD Member Book, No. FY11-3 (Dec. 2010, P). ASCD Member Books mail to Premium (P), Select (S), and Institutional Plus (I+) members on this schedule: Jan., PSI+; Feb., P; Apr., PSI+; May, P; July, PSI+; Aug., P; Sept., PSI+; Nov., PSI+; Dec., P. Select membership was formerly known as Comprehensive membership.

Quantity discounts for the paperback edition only: 10–49 copies, 10%; 50+ copies, 15%; for 1,000 or more copies, call 800-933-2723, ext. 5634, or 703-575-5634. For desk copies: member@ascd.org.

PAPERBACK ISBN: 978-1-4166-1091-5   ASCD product #109041
Also available as an e-book (see Books in Print for the ISBNs).

Library of Congress Cataloging-in-Publication Data

Zmuda, Allison.

 Breaking free from myths about teaching and learning : innovation as an engine for student success / Allison Zmuda.

   p. cm.

 Includes bibliographical references and index.

 ISBN 978-1-4166-1091-5 (pbk. : alk. paper) 1. School improvement programs--United States. 2. Academic achievement—United States. 3. Educational leadership--United States. I. Title.

 LB2822.82.Z68 2010

 371.207—dc22

               2010035631

20 19 18 17 16 15 14 13 12 11 10   1 2 3 4 5 6 7 8 9 10 11 12

For Diane Ullman — My friend, my soul sister, my champion. You ruined me for other bosses.

breaking
free
from myths about
teaching and learning

Acknowledgments

First and foremost, I want to thank my children, Cuda James Zmuda and Zoe Ann Zmuda, for their daily testament to what learning is supposed to feel like. This book is my attempt to more deeply understand how to be a better parent, educator, and community leader so that the schools they attend and the endeavors they pursue embrace their spirit, grow their talent, and deepen their determination.

My development editor, Scott Willis, has supported me throughout the entire writing process. When I was afraid the book was too weird, too depressing, too naive, or too inaccessible, he gave me the encouragement I needed to continue the struggle. He helped me to trust my voice and my words even when we both weren't sure where it was headed.

Over the past years, I have been blessed to have mentors who have taught me so much about the nature of learning:

- Jay McTighe, who has listened to me ramble about this book for several years and patiently helped me uncover what I truly wanted to say;
- Grant Wiggins, who held me accountable to say something new and to have the courage to commit to new ideas;
- Charlie Kiefer and Annika Schahn, who revealed to me the nature of thought, the power of insight, and the joy that is possible in every moment;
- Diane Ullman and Delores Bolton, who have helped me fly and kept me grounded;

- Ilyon Woo, who has spent years pouring her heart, soul, and mind into telling one powerful story to deepen our humanity;
- Susan Epstein, who modeled for me throughout my life that you can make a career out of pursuing your dreams; and
- Paul Fisher, who believed in me from my post-stroke beginning that I could and will get my language back.

As an education consultant, I have been fortunate to collaborate with educators, community members, and students who are determined to make school a more valuable experience for everyone. Listed below are those partners who have inspired me to write this book.

- The curriculum and instructional leadership team of Virginia Beach City Public Schools—Marie Balen, Joe Burnsworth, Christine Caskey, and Pat Konopnicki—have blazed so many important trails that have elevated the assessment and instructional practices throughout the division. In addition, the articulation of 21st century skills and accompanying continuum by Jared Cotton and a powerful group of staff and community members brought substantive clarity that will support Compass 2015. Finally, to the Candid Conversations about Race team members, especially Frances Thompson, who have taught me more about humanity, decency, resilience, and compassion than anyone else. Their personal and professional courage is remarkable and serves as a reminder of how far we've come and how far we still have to go.
- The leadership team and staff of Grayslake Community High School District 127 in Illinois, for their collective commitment to one another in the design of school goals and accompanying curriculum. Special thanks to Assistant Superintendent Scott Fech for his perseverance, heart, and leadership; he encourages students and staff alike to pursue the vision of what's possible instead of becoming depressed by challenges.
- The Greenwich Secondary Review Committee, the leadership team of the middle and high schools, and district curriculum leaders for their countless hours of conversations on what the goals of school should be, how to best frame goals-related language, and what policies, practices, and plans must be revised in light of goals. Special thanks to

Chris Winters for his tireless efforts to keep all of us focused on what's most important.

- Superintendent of Nanuet Public Schools Mark McNeill and Superintendent of Croton-Harmon Ed Fuhrman sat down with me and "dreamed big" because of their deep-seated belief that there was "something more" that needed to be done to make education more meaningful for everyone. It was a joy to imagine the possibilities with them.

- Superintendent Laurie Kimbrel, the Board of Trustees, and the staff of Tamalpais Union High School District in California. They are a talented, fascinating, powerful group of people who pursue individual and collective ways to make learning more meaningful and relevant for all children. The conversations around the development of the mission statement, learning principles, and curriculum development have shown that a diverse group of people can arrive at powerful conclusions about what learning should be.

- Kerri Nelson, Superintendent of South Tama County Community School District in Iowa, is a shining star in the new generation of leadership who exhibits the fortitude, vision, and passion needed to improve the quality of schooling.

- Director of Curriculum Lori Rapp and Assistant Superintendent Penny Reddell of Lewisville ISD in Texas for their steadfast, principled leadership of a massive curriculum development effort. Their efforts have made it possible for staff to articulate learning priorities and develop powerful assessments to ensure that all students will be successful.

- The outstanding work of Carrollton-Farmers Branch ISD curriculum leaders John David, Tanya Garvey, Pam Smith, and Erica Ysbrand. Their ability to design for "the big picture" has improved the quality of assessment and instructional practices throughout the system. Thank you to Holly Barber and Sheila Maher for their trust in all of us to do this important work.

- Principal Adam Johnson and Hartford Law and Government Academy staff for their courage to define rigorous goals for their students so that they not only have the tools to personally succeed, but just as importantly provide the next generation of leadership to improve the larger community.

- The curriculum leadership team of Milford Public Schools in Milford, Connecticut: Mike Cummings, Gail Krois, Carol Malone, and department coordinators. Their work over the past several years has been tremendous in its scope, impact, and sincerity.

- The school leadership team of Mariana Bracetti Academy Charter School: Andrew Boglioli, Adrienne Davids, Chuck Priestly, and Jana Somma. Their commitment to students and staff is an inspiration. It is rare to have a full complement of leaders who are relentless in growing the capacity of staff, students, and themselves.

- The staff and school leaders of the Upper Grand District School Board in Ontario, Canada. It has been a pleasure to think and work with them on how to improve the effectiveness of schools so that students are truly engaged. Special thanks to Pat Hamilton, Erin Kelly, Darryl Kirkland, Brent McDonald, and Tim Murray for their unfailing support, friendship, humor, and lame book titles during the writing process.

- Dani Thibodeau, the Executive Director of Education Connection, for her commitment to and passion for providing vital services to children, families, and adults so that they can soar.

- The dedicated leaders of teaching and learning I had the privilege of working with in Grand Island Public Schools, Nebraska: Sue Burch, Steve Burkholder, Deb Harder, Deb Karle, Nancy Schisler, and Mary Unger. Their intensity, dedication, and vision not only grew the quality of work within their system but has served as a model for so many others.

- The original Teaching and Learning crew at CREC–Cathy Horton, Peggy Neal, and Diana Roberge. They demonstrated how teacher-leaders can rise up and grow the capacity of their colleagues and themselves. Those were the best staff meetings I ever attended because of the depth of your thinking and your passion for the work.

Finally, to my husband and best friend, Tom Zmuda. He has been my support system through this entire experience. His own journey to rediscover what is possible has been an endless source of inspiration and strength for me. I am truly grateful to have married the best teacher I have ever met.

Introduction

This book is my response to the pervasive weariness I have observed during numerous classroom observations, staff development workshops, and leadership meetings. Despite intentions to ensure that all learners can be successful, educators seem to be working harder than ever but accomplishing less, while students seem to be more disengaged than ever but longing for more. In the effort to improve student achievement, we have pushed the existing system of schools into hyperdrive, asking students and staff to work at a speed that negatively affects learning in the long run. Limitations on what is possible in schools are generated and perpetuated by the very people who suffer because of them. The more certain we are that schools cannot change, the more awful the situation becomes for everyone.

This book is a call to action for teachers, departments, school staff, educational leaders, community activists, school board members, and students. The premise of this book is that school is not working—not for students, who are more bored and disengaged; not for teachers or administrators, who are worn down from serving more purposes; not for college professors, who need to do more remediation with incoming students; and not for employers, who are more deeply concerned about the quality of prospective applicants than ever before.

For schools to work better, we need to break free from myths about teaching and learning and find ways to "hardwire" schools to develop the natural intelligence of our learners. This conversation cannot be layered on top of the pile of existing implementation efforts to improve student achievement. It requires the courage, tenacity, and certitude that our schools can become true learning organizations. We need to stop rushing to action, stop killing new ideas, and stop resigning ourselves to doing the best we can with the system we have. It is time to focus on the problems of 21st century life that we have been too busy to acknowledge and find power in the opportunity to redefine the work of our schools. The mission of a 21st century learning organization is to engage all learners in the acquisition of key knowledge and skills and the development of connections so that they can pursue powerful questions, tackle complex problems, collaborate with diverse people, imagine new possibilities, and communicate their ideas.

As you read this book, be patient with me (and with yourselves), because there are no quick-fix solutions or fail-proof strategies. There is also no sweeping condemnation of schools, educators, children, or society. Fads, flying accusations, and rush to action have gotten us nowhere. In fact, much of the push for developing 21st century skills is eerily similar to earlier attempts to reform education. The novelty of this book lies in a multifaceted exploration of the problem. While some facets are likely to be more familiar (and perhaps more intriguing) than others, I encourage you to consider the possibility that new connections and fresh thinking lie in the creative recombination of the knowledge already in your head. The "next big thing" could be the idea that schools must finally become the learning organizations that we entrust with nourishing the hearts and minds of our students and ourselves.

Chapter 1 explores the disconnect of students from their schooling as demonstrated by their minimum-compliance attitudes, disengagement, and lack of motivation. At young ages, students construct generalizations about what school requires of them as learners; simply put, these generalizations are wrong. In their efforts to do well in school, students have largely become low-level bureaucrats who complete the requisite paperwork but suffer from the monotony of the experience. While the myths explored in Chapter 1 may reflect flawed conceptions of learning, they are understandable coping mechanisms given the design of curriculum, assessment, and instruction. Not only do these realities dampen the enjoyment of learning, but they also harm students' abilities to become wiser and more skillful, to persevere in the face of challenges, and to apply their learning to new problems and contexts. These concerns about the performance of our students also pertain to our performance as educators, making it difficult to get teachers to believe in the sincerity or potential of any improvement effort.

Spinning off of the long-standing concern about the disconnect between the learner and the school, Chapter 2 explores two problems that have evolved over the years. First, the demands on 21st century workers and citizens constitute a shift in the way students are expected to think, work, and interact with others in the real world, yet the instructional core in many classrooms remains teacher-directed and highly routinized. Second, the way time is organized in and out of school, leading to a never-ending list of assignments and tasks for students to accomplish, inhibits deep learning. Accordingly, the defining documents, practices, and assessments at the heart of many school structures benefit neither the performance of our children during their time in school nor their success after graduation day.

Chapter 3 shifts the focus from the limitations of our current reality toward what could be: a 21st century schoolhouse that is truly a learning organization. Through the development of mission and vision statements, we can create a new image of what learning goals we aspire to achieve and what practices, policies, and structures will make that work most meaningful for our learners. This section includes exemplars developed by informal and formal school leadership teams to illustrate possibilities and inspire your work.

Chapter 4 explores how to measure and motivate student achievement through the design of authentic tasks. When students are invited to apply their prior knowledge and personal interests to solve relevant problems and communicate their thinking, they can experience real enjoyment. Creativity is an essential component of task design in a 21st century school. While marginalized and misunderstood by many, creativity is fundamental to modern life, as it requires both deep knowledge and playful use of that knowledge to create new connections, products, solution paths, and forms of expression.

Chapter 5 delves into the science of learning to better understand the impact of our structures, practices, and policies on the learner. Through the development and establishment of learning principles, educators can transform their daily practices to better align with how the brain works and, consequently, how learners learn. Research also proves helpful as we discuss four common practices that *don't* work: relying on extrinsic motivators, praising students' intelligence, tolerating disengagement, and lowering expectations. The intent of this discussion is to engender greater engagement and purpose in our students and ourselves.

Chapter 6 revisits the myths delineated in Chapter 1 and provides concrete suggestions to enable new realities to emerge. These ideas are intended to open up the reader's thinking about both small-scale and sweeping reforms, thus beginning to change the relationship between the learner and the learning organization so that it becomes a more natural, energizing experience for all.

What Does This Text Require of the Writer and the Reader?

This book is an act of combinatory play for both writer and reader. It is the pursuit of cutting-edge ideas and eternal wisdom, the commitment to improve schools for our students and ourselves, and the passion for creativity and deep knowledge. The list of references cited is certainly eclectic; one area of exploration led to another in a way that broke the boundaries of traditional education literature. Experts in business, dance, creativity, neuroscience, meditation, psychology, and innovative design add dimension to conversations about the development of ideas and the substance of learning.

This book is also an act of courage for both writer and reader. It requires the suspension of what you may know for certain, the broadmindedness to explore areas that may be beyond your current expertise, and the search for connectivity among areas that previously felt unrelated. As a consultant, I have the privilege to work with educators in very different systems, with unique challenges, diverse student populations, and limited resources. Despite the commitment to do what's best for students, it is increasingly apparent that there is a crisis of confidence and imagination among educators. They often describe what is impossible with such detail, passion, and certainty that there is little space for new ideas to breathe. They rapidly draw upon extensive expertise and past practices in their memory banks to justify, explain, and deny reality. To begin to break the "certainty habit," I have integrated reflection questions and quotations throughout the text to slow down your thinking, for the reality we think we see in schools is both triggered by and confirmed by our thinking. The brief texts, quotations, and questions in italics are intended to forestall action or judgment. Try it now as you consider the following three statements from three very different authorities on the nature of thought.

We see only what we know.

Goethe

I can live with doubt and uncertainty and not knowing. I have approximate answers and possible beliefs and different degrees of certainty about different things. . . . It doesn't frighten me.

Nobel laureate Richard Feynman

Our minds have their own agendas. We can intervene through greater understanding of what we can and cannot control, by knowing where potential deceptions lurk, and by a willingness to accept that our knowledge of the world around us is limited by fundamental conflicts in how our minds work. . . . Certainty is not biologically possible. We must learn (and teach our children) to tolerate the unpleasantness of uncertainty.

Neurologist Richard Burton (2008, p. 223)

I am regularly baffled by the certainty with which educators tell me what can and can't be done, what the system permits and disallows, and what students are capable of and have no shot at becoming. So many educators are resigned about what schooling has to be because they cannot see it for what it is: a set of habits that feel permanent but do not have permanence. We were not predestined for a system of Carnegie units, standardized tests, and grade-level expectations. For just a little while, turn your back on your certainty and instead make space for the possibility that there must be a better way to "do" school, a way that requires—but also creates—tremendous energy.

The reflection questions in each chapter are intended to open up thinking about unexamined habits, assumptions, and practices within the school that inhibit learning. Ideally, these questions will become fodder for dialogue, insight, and new practice. They can be thought through in structured venues, such as professional learning community meetings, or in less controlled environments, such as teaching blogs or personal journals. Spend a few minutes playing with one or more of the following questions. Try not to push yourself to come up with an answer, but rather observe the train of feelings and thoughts that cross your mind.

Reflection Questions:

What do students think about during the school day because of how we design learning?

How do those thoughts help students grow? How do they limit students?

How much has the work in your school changed in the past two decades? Have those changes led to increased engagement?

What is the most innovative idea that has improved the thinking (and the resulting work) of staff? Of students?

What current practices are off limits in reimagining the work of the school?

If a reflection question unsettles you or others with whom you are sharing this reading experience, it may be better to acknowledge the discomfort than to aggressively pursue it in that moment. I have found while writing this book that there are times where it is either excruciating or unproductive to engage with certain questions. But I have also learned to come back to those questions periodically to see if something has changed or something new has occurred to me that opens up space for inquiry to begin. The only wrong way to treat these questions, or this text for that matter, is as an intellectual exercise tangential to the "real work" of schools. The quality of the reader's thinking throughout this experience affects the depth of the connections to one's own learning organization.

I believe in the following ideas:

- Learning is a joyful experience when it commands our attention.
- Schools can transform into learning organizations the moment that you decide there must be a better way, and then pursue it.
- What we think defines the quality of our experience.
- Exploring unfamiliar territories creates the uncertainty and discomfort needed to begin to think anew.
- The power of educators to affect the lives of children is breathtaking.

I wish you the best of luck on this journey; I am on it with you. I have struggled for over two years to find words to express what I have always known to be true.

I'll see you in the Afterword.

1

Myths Related to
Learning in Schools

*It is little short of a miracle that modern methods of instruction have
not completely strangled the holy curiosity of inquiry.*

Albert Einstein

Reflection Question

Is fundamental change possible given the myths our culture holds
related to schooling?

This chapter focuses on the intellectual stultification of learners, the first
of three fundamental problems that limit the quality of thinking and
efficacy of the educational experience. Students in increasingly lower
grades and educators at increasingly earlier points in their careers lose
their joy for their work. They become jaded by the limitations on their
imaginations, frustrated by the questions they are not allowed to pursue,
and depressed by the more experienced peers around them who seem
uninterested in their ideas. Somewhere along the way, we—educators,
parents, and students alike—decided that schooling was supposed to

feel this way, that the drudgery of school was necessary in order for learning to happen. We are all culpable for perpetuating this reality.

I am not the first educator to come to the conclusion that schools that prize efficiency over development of learners' intelligence will fail to truly educate. In fact, approximately 100 years ago, pedagogical progressives championed this philosophy as part of larger educational reform. John Dewey and his colleagues railed against an industrial formulation of education that prized organizational efficiency of knowledge over thinking, reflection, and the development of democratic ideals. These progressives put forth the notion that schools should respect the natural diversity of the individual learners as a basis for instruction and train their minds so that they could become engaged citizens. While the problem may be a long-standing one, it is exacerbated by the fact that the deficiencies of school as a learning organization have become more pronounced.

[Each of us is born into this world full of wonder, curiosity, creativity, and dreams] From their first days of life, children begin to develop their capacity to explore and make sense of their surroundings, to bond with those who care for them, and to experience the joy of being alive. The way they experience the world becomes their "original research" and the basis for the conclusions they draw. When their formal schooling begins, their natural tendencies to learn are largely supplanted by the routines developed to organize their play and build basic skills. These routines train students to follow directions, be respectful of their peers, make predictions, and accumulate knowledge. These routines also, however, send a quiet message that learning is a predictable process managed by the teacher. Students quickly figure out that there are rules to the classroom, that kids are sorted based on ability, that there are right answers and wrong answers, and that there are ways to make their teachers happy.

This chapter explores how these early generalizations become pervasive myths that estrange students from their natural capacity to learn. Failure becomes a bad word and is to be avoided at all costs. Giving the teacher what he or she wants is critical if you want to get good grades. Questions are good only if they are on topic. Developing good ideas must be done in accordance with the directions. Students soon become more comfortable responding to questions with straightforward answers, solving problems that require a predictable solution path, producing writing according to a given template, and conducting research by collecting facts on teacher-determined topics. Intrinsic motivation, joy, and purpose are replaced by apathy, fixation on grades, and commitment to "do what it takes" to make teachers and parents happy. Many students come to believe that school is a tedious enterprise to be endured, and they live for those moments when the parameters are removed and they are once again their own masters. The result—boredom and lackluster achievement—is not surprising, but is this type of schooling necessary for students to acquire the knowledge they need to do well in postsecondary education programs? The final part of this chapter briefly explores the issue of college readiness and how the aggressive pace of curricula and measurement of discrete knowledge and skills do not translate into postsecondary education success.

Students are not alone in their struggle to learn. Consider classroom teachers as learners. They enter the profession with deep knowledge of a subject or range of subjects and a passion to work with children. But once they are hired, they are not required to learn about the course content they teach; such learning is voluntary, most frequently occurring as part of a master's or doctoral program, a community book group, or a grant-funded project. In contrast, learning about the *profession* is mandatory. Such learning experiences, however, often depress the quality of thinking, level of creativity, and optimism of staff. On an annual basis, the teacher is introduced to a new area of focus that will improve student achievement. The assumption is that if the individual adds this layer to existing practice, then students will benefit. With little clarity about the reason behind the area of focus and even less clarity about how to find the time to do this work on top of everything else, the teacher dutifully attempts to learn. The sincerity of learning, the joy of learning, and the purpose of learning are missing, but the attempt is made in response to professional expectations. Regardless of how interesting or powerful the learning experience could be, it is clear to all that the focus will be short-lived as this topic will be replaced by the next new thing. This pattern is as pervasive as it is dysfunctional. It is openly discussed by staff and administrators alike, but rarely examined as a habitual collection of choices that could be set aside in search for a better way of professional learning.

Acting on Myths

My conversations with thousands of students from my time as teacher, consultant, and parent have revealed a number of beliefs that are widely accepted in our schools; nine of these are detailed below. I describe each in terms of the effect it has on student thinking and explore the reasons many teachers deliberately or unconsciously perpetuate it.

Whether these beliefs are born from experience, comments from other students, misguided comparison of students' own performance with their peers, or feedback from family members and teachers, adhering to them reduces learners' engagement level, perceived capacity, and resilience. The stories students tell themselves about what kind of learners they are, what it takes for them to do well, and whether or not such success is desirable persists through years of schooling with minimal interruption or acknowledgment from the adults. By revealing and examining these myths, I hope to stir up sincere concerns about their pervasiveness in your own classrooms and inspire you to think about other tacit beliefs at work in your school. It is time to engage our students in honest conversations about what it feels like (and what it *should* feel like) to learn.

Myth #1: The rules of this classroom and subject area are determined by each teacher.

Many students see classroom rules, protocols, scoring tools, and performance expectations as driven by the *teacher's* personal choice about how to structure the learning environment. This perception is profoundly different from seeing them as expectations driven by a specific *discipline*—what professionals in the field do to create, develop, and analyze ideas and information; produce quality work; and communicate effectively with others.

Classroom teachers have tremendous freedom to structure the protocols, grading policies, and expectations for their classrooms. This individualization often goes well beyond the creation of classroom rules and routines—it includes what texts and topics are studied in depth, how student grades are calculated, what type of contribution is welcomed during class discussions, the extent to which technology tools are integrated into the classroom, whether students are required to conduct research, and how much homework is necessary to further student development. These are substantive instructional choices that have profound impact on what and how students learn.

While the proliferation of districtwide and schoolwide curriculum and pacing guides, core assessments, and (where applicable) state standards and testing has limited the extent of this individualization, many teachers continue to advocate for more personal autonomy, not less. One teacher explained to me, "Who would know better than I what is appropriate for the children I teach? I'm the one who knows them best; I'm the one who knows what's possible. Anyone who tries to do that for me not only will likely make everyone perform worse, but also is disrespecting my professionalism."

The problem with this line of reasoning is that it assumes that if good people with good intentions are each independently trusted to do their work, then everything will turn out fine. To the contrary, in order for the design of learning to be meaningful for the learners, it must stem from their prior knowledge, personal experiences, and current challenges. When continuity from year to year or topic to topic is not maintained, students become "blank slates" for their teachers to fill with new knowledge. The problem with the blank slate mentality is that students get accustomed to wiping the slate clean to prepare for next year's (or next day's) learning experiences. This willingness to learn anew becomes a liability; students lose the ability to apply what they have previously learned to make sense of new information, develop new connections, and tackle new problems.

Teachers lament this mentality—"Why can't students remember what we did last week?"—but express little hope of changing learning conditions. Coherence of curricular aims within and across disciplines, consistent feedback mechanisms, and models of quality work create clarity of expectations. When educators can achieve consensus not only about learning priorities but also about how such priorities are measured and what criteria define successful work, students can stop fixating on the personality at the front of the room and start focusing on the task at hand.

Myth #2: What the teacher wants me to say is more important than what I want to say.

Students come to believe that if they can figure out what the teacher wants, likes, and thinks, they will succeed in the class. Many have learned to stifle their own points of view, ideas, creative impulses, and problem-solving approaches, deeming them unworthy of pursuit. Students who adopt this way of thinking often elicit direction from the teacher to ensure that their work "fits" what the teacher wants:

- "What do you think a good color choice would be?"
- "What do you see when you look at the data?"
- "What do you think is important to remember here?"
- "What do you think the author means in this passage?"
- "What do you think is the best way to approach the problem?"

This customer-service mentality is fundamentally different from working to produce a quality result. The job of a learner is not to please the teacher in order to get "paid" (through praise, good grades, a diploma), but rather to grow one's own capacity. In the following passage, Dana, a 10th grader, shares her insight about how passive she had become.

> It's easy to take what the teacher says and regurgitate it without even thinking about what was said, and it's how we've been taught to learn. When I set out to write this paragraph, I actually thought I should ask my teacher to spell out what he wanted me to write. . . . If I tried to challenge my teacher, all it would take is a little bit of him pushing back to make me drop my argument and look like a deer in the headlights, even if I had a decent argument. Now that I know how passive I've been, I'm ready to make some changes in my learning style.

When students back away from their own opinions or points of view because of intellectual pressure or authoritative control, they learn to defer to the expert (and, perhaps even worse, to stop trying to develop arguments altogether). Colin, another 10th grader, wrote to me about his frustration with how he was taught to write by his teachers.

> When I was first asked to write an essay or paragraph, I was given an "outline" where you wrote your topic sentence, filled in some body sentences, and then closed it with a "clincher" or summarizing sentence. I can understand the purpose and usefulness of this outline for originally learning how to write a good paragraph. Time after time in 4th grade, 5th grade, and so on up until 8th grade, I kept on seeing this basic format that you had to write by. . . . In 8th grade I began to get bored with almost all of my subjects because we had to do no thinking. Everything was "spoon fed" to us, as my English teacher would say. I decided to start doing things my way and thinking outside the box. I know that I am not a good writer, but when I get an idea I think about it and stick with it even though it may not agree with the format.

Colin's statements derive from years of school experiences where students are expected to take notes on key points made in class, follow procedures clearly delineated by the teacher in order to gain the maximum number of points, and participate in class discussions framed by questions designed to review content material. One student described her job as a learner as doing "bad karaoke" of what the teacher already thinks. Another described learning as "going down a path walking in someone else's footsteps." A third student stated, "If the students had more to say in what they think, then the teachers might learn more of what they think instead of just saying that they're right or wrong. If we had more of an opinion, the teachers might learn more of what we think of certain things and could make their lessons more interesting so they could have more engaged learners."

This passivity erodes student engagement and achievement over time, making it difficult for many students to reawaken their minds and voices to develop profound questions, big ideas, innovative approaches, and creative expressions when given the opportunity. While teaching students structure and appropriate mechanics does matter, there has to be a balance between an emphasis on the rules and an emphasis on the development of ideas.

Myth #3: The point of an assignment is to get it done so that it's off the to-do list.

Students who believe this axiom typically feel as if they are drowning in work—there are always more problems, more readings, and more tasks to complete. They become overwhelmed by the volume of work and the scarcity of time, feeling significant stress about how to manage the completion of their assignments. One student described how lack of time undermines personal connection to an assignment: "Most students just do the assignment because there is not time to really study it. We don't really get a chance to go further into the parts of the topic we are studying that aren't a part of the curriculum because we have already moved to a whole new topic." It is an understandable coping mechanism to work quickly, get it done, and hope it goes well.

The glut of assignments is intended not to punish the learner but to provide necessary practice to meet local, state, and national expectations. However, the effectiveness of a practice is determined by its impact on student learning. What if students benefited from the assignments only if they were engaged in the work? In the spring of 2009, the Canadian Council on Learning (CCL) reviewed 18 studies of homework research conducted from 2003 to 2007. (The full report can be accessed online at www.ccl-cca.ca/CCL/Reports/LessonsInLearning/LinL200900430Homework.htm.) Here are several of their key findings:

• There was no evidence to suggest that the general rule of thumb that the amount of assigned homework at the end of the school day should not exceed 10 minutes per grade level was invalid.

• Homework has different effects on various groups of students. Those most likely to benefit from homework were older students (8th grade and above) and lower-achieving students.

• Homework is more likely to be effective when students are actively engaged with it. Such engagement may stem from a metacognitive component, in which students make their own decisions on how best to approach a problem or task.

While research into the correlation between homework and achievement has always been complex, these findings confirm what many students and teachers would describe as "common sense." When students intently focus on an assignment and invest time in explaining their thinking and reflecting on the process, their achievement will likely improve. When students are given more work than they can reasonably complete, they will take shortcuts to get it done or compromise other areas of their physical and emotional health (lack of sleep, use of stimulants, increased levels of stress), which may only minimally improve (and in some cases harm) achievement—and most certainly will sap their enthusiasm for school learning. It is important to separate our professional urgency for students to score well on standardized and local assessments from our responsibility to accomplish learning goals.

Myth #4: If I make a mistake, my job is only to replace it with the right answer.

Students who think this way routinely erase incorrect answers during class work or homework reviews and replace them with the correct answers. These students do not attempt to learn what went wrong in the original attempt or to confirm whether, in fact, their response was a legitimate alternative approach. This routine of "erase and replace" limits not only the value of homework assignments but also the value of more substantive tasks. For example, when a student completes a rough draft of a writing assignment, he or she expects the teacher to circle the mechanical errors for correction and is usually happy to fix them, but more complicated marks (a squiggle under a sentence that is unclear, for example) are typically ignored by the student as there is no visible flaw identified or no obvious remedy. A student who operates under this belief expects that when an art teacher gives feedback on the use of shading in the student's work, that it is the teacher's responsibility to pick up a charcoal pencil to help remedy the problem.

While many teachers are irritated by students' lack of willingness to examine errors and grow from feedback, they enable that behavior by continuing to fix many of their problems for them. Some teachers do so out of a real concern that lack of willingness to help will be perceived as lack of caring. Other teachers continue to do work for students because it is more expedient. It can be quite time-consuming to examine the nature of an error. Still other teachers work to improve the piece instead of working to improve the capacity of the writer who produced it; they fix the sentence structure instead of reteaching mechanics. Ultimately, this belief will remain in place as long as the quick fix of providing the right answer is more expedient for teachers.

[Creating substantive opportunities for students to improve their work is only half of the problem; the other half is dependent upon students' engagement with tasks in the first place.] If the task that students are given is a response to an uninspired writing prompt that is measured by whether it follows basic structural rules or a set of problems that requires execution of a single solution path to achieve a single right answer, it is unreasonable to expect students to muster enthusiasm for the endeavor. When the work is not meaningful to begin with, revision simply becomes another item on the to-do list. Students must become more connected to their schoolwork through sustained focus on a select number of meaningful tasks. (This topic will be discussed further in Chapter 4.)

Myth #5: I feel proud of myself only if I receive a good grade.

[Students use grades to identify and sort themselves as learners: being a straight-*A* student becomes an identity, not just a grade point average.] Students also use grades to discern their current and future capacity in a subject area: "I got an *F* in science, but that's okay because I know that I am not good at it." "I got a *B* on my essay, but I always get *B*s, no matter how hard I try." Often, students only glance at the comments that accompany their grades (if they read them at all), even though this explicit feedback is the most time-consuming for teachers to communicate as well as a powerful tool for students to use to improve their performance on similar tasks. One high school student explained to me, "If we get a bad grade on something, we automatically jump to the fact that we can't do that particular thing. We don't think, 'Well, I got that right, so I must be improving.' We just conclude that we can't do it and feel lower than other students who got better grades."

Some teachers I have spoken with would take this belief a step further. They contend that students view grades not as a description of their achievement, but rather as an end in and of itself. They lament the fact that students appear more interested in maximizing the points they earned than in learning the ideas, logic, skills, or information central to the task. Thomas Guskey and Jane Bailey (2001) suggest that grades in fact do become a commodity:

> Around the middle school years and sometimes earlier . . . students no longer see grades as a source of feedback to guide improvements in their learning. Instead, they regard grades as the major commodity teachers and schools have to offer in exchange for their performance. This change brings a slow but steady shift in students' focus away from learning toward what they must do to obtain the grade commodity. . . . That is why, for example, the first questions students ask when a teacher announces an upcoming project or event are 'Does it count?' and 'How many points is it worth?' Teachers' answers to these questions give students a clear idea of how much importance they should attach to that particular event. (pp. 18–19)

In Chapter 5, I will discuss in greater depth how the use of grades and other rewards as extrinsic motivation limits success. For now, it is fair to surmise that students use grades in ways that are quite dysfunctional: they either see the score as an indicator of their intelligence or as a sign of their ability to play the game of school. Grades must become more transparent measures of true achievement that provide students and parents with good information about current performance in order to improve future performance.

Myth #6: Speed is synonymous with intelligence.

Students who hold this belief watch other students finish first and become envious. "Why can't I be finished already, too?" they wonder. Often these students either try to work at a pace that is unnatural for them—too quickly to focus on the details, nuances, development, and mechanics of the task—or they work at their own pace but berate themselves for being slow or stupid. This generalization is further magnified when students feel little connection to the work that they are doing in the first place (see Myths #2 and #9). Learning can become tedious when stripped of its playfulness and passion, and students begin to operate on automatic pilot or at an artificial speed.

Students are not alone in this race: their teachers operate at an even more relentless pace. Teachers validate this belief in their rush to "cover" an untenably long list of content topics, skills, and strategies before a test date or before the end of the school year. I distinctly remember walking down the hallway behind two high school math teachers around 10:00 a.m. on the first day of school. One teacher complained to the other that she was already "hopelessly behind" because she hadn't had a chance to give students their homework assignment, which meant that tomorrow's lesson wouldn't work. That problem was compounded by the short schedule on the following day for a school pep rally and a short week for the first week of school. "That means this week is already over, putting me one week behind already," she worried. This level of time pressure is absurd. How is it healthy for teachers to be "behind" within three hours of the start of the school year?

Not only does this mythical rapid pace cause significant stress in both teachers and students, it also creates rigidity in their minds and dialogues. The pressures to prepare students for standardized tests and curricular exams as well as the pressure to finish the curriculum over the course of the year makes it difficult for teachers to welcome alternate points of view, interpretations, ways of communicating, and solution paths. In the desire to be more expedient, teachers are too busy to be supportive of the natural inefficiency of learning—figuring it out in your own way, in your own words, on your own schedule. Students who are quick to get the answer or who demonstrate fluency with a procedure become models for the rest of the class; they provide relief and a sense of satisfaction that perhaps covering the curriculum in the time allotted is possible, at least for some.

Speed pressure also causes teachers to be less willing to entertain "good ideas" in staff development. They are so focused on the calendar and what they still have to do that any innovative or inspiring idea becomes "one more thing" to add to an already overloaded schedule. There must be ample space in the classroom for teachers and students to learn inefficiently—"elbow room" to explore interesting tangents, compare points of view, and consider alternate solution paths.

Myth #7: If I get too far behind, I will never catch up.

Students who believe this assume that teachers and other students label them: "He's one of the slow ones." "She tries hard but doesn't really get it." "He's just not that smart." They also believe that teachers sort, group, and schedule them differently than other students. They think that teachers are giving them easier work, which only widens the gap between them and their peers. Without necessary space in pacing guides, unit designs, or school schedule, students who work at a slower pace become difficult to teach. While their struggles may be normal given the complexity of the subject matter, lack of prior knowledge, or disconnect with personal frame of reference, the further behind a student becomes, the more frustrating he or she is to teach. It isn't personal; it's just that there is so much to do within the given school year that the task of remediation becomes untenable. Some teachers openly wonder whether students who are too far behind should even be in their classrooms: "How can I be expected to teach them 4th grade math if they didn't learn what they needed to last year?" Other teachers wonder whether it is fair to expect students who are struggling to meet the same expectations as the rest of the class: "Isn't it mean-spirited to hold students accountable to an expectation they can't meet?" When time is packed too tightly, a small rough patch or a bad marking period can quickly snowball into much more serious academic problems. Once again, there must be ample space in the classroom for students to struggle, to not get it, or to be behind without such struggles turning into an instant crisis.

Myth #8: The way I want to be seen by my class-mates affects the way I conduct myself as a learner.

Students who think this way project an image of what learning is like for them that may or may not reflect their genuine experience. Students and teachers alike become accustomed to the character the learner plays with little consideration as to its authenticity. It is fascinating, however, how learners change their role in certain classrooms because of the subject matter, the teacher, or the models set by the students around them. A student may be slumped in his or her seat for an entire class period, and then become an energetic participant in the next class. Many teachers simply accept the student in front of them as "the real student" instead of wondering about what motivates that particular learner and whether the behaviors they observe are the exception or the norm. Teachers may also forget how the classroom becomes a stage where the scenes enacted are less about the content of the plot and more about the dynamics of human relationships.

Appearances can be deceiving. The nonchalant attitude a student exhibits may mask the real effort invested in completing a task or preparing for a test. Detachment during class discussions and small-group tasks may mask real insecurity about whether a student believes he or she has something smart or interesting to contribute. An aggressive attempt to take control of a conversation or a group assignment may cover up a real fear of getting a bad grade or worry about being seen as less intelligent than others. Regardless of what is going on with students at or beneath the surface, the job of the teacher is to draw out learners so that engagement is possible. It is likely that the terms and the degree of engagement are different for every learner, but engagement affects the quality and potential joy of learning, making it a nonnegotiable goal.

Myth #9: What I'm learning in school doesn't have much to do with my life, but it isn't supposed to —it's school.

Students who think this way have resigned themselves to the idea that school is boring. School is what happens in between more meaningful learning experiences, such as communicating with friends, researching topics of personal interest, and learning how to solve authentic problems in their own lives. A young woman explained to me, "I feel sometimes that I just really need to get the homework or project done. It is hard to really get into what I am doing because most of the projects and homework that I do don't interest me, but I know that I need to have them for later on in life." Straight-A students and failing students alike may tell this tale; their performance is based on the extent to which they have made peace with this belief.

Teachers and parents often defer curricular relevance to "someday"—someday when you go to college, when you have bills to pay, when you are in charge of your own reading selections, when you can select your own career, when you can create your masterpiece, when you start your own business, this learning will be relevant. But what's the likelihood that what students learn in school will still be accessible if they never commit themselves to learning in the first place? If students do not create cognitive structures to flexibly store and access knowledge (establishing patterns, creating connections, and so on), their years of schooling will likely be of little use when "someday" finally does show up.

Effect of Teaching and Learning Myths on Life and Work in School

When students are bored with the work they are asked to do, they superficially read texts, casually execute procedures, and cursorily explain their thinking. If students do not experience flow (see the work of Mihaly Csikszentmihalyi) and do not regularly work in the zone of proximal development, they become acculturated to the boredom generated by the nine myths explored in this chapter. This detachment makes it increasingly difficult for students to retain learning after the lesson, unit, or year is over, and harder for teachers to improve student performance. Listen in on a virtual conversation among commenters on a blog I discovered by typing "bored in school" into the Google search engine (the blog post in question can be found at www.takingchildrenseriously .com/sooooo_bored_in_school):

> *Comment:* I used to liven up lessons by drawing a grid with one space for each minute, and coloring them in as the minutes passed.
>
> *Comment:* LOL, I had other kill-the-time games as well. It amazes and saddens me to reflect on how much of my irreplaceable life was wasted that way.
>
> *Comment:* The point of school is to learn to cope with boredom? . . . I can't say that my school-endurance skills have served me well in adult life. Meetings at work, for instance, are much harder because of the school-inculcated reflex to zone out and become lost in my own thoughts. School didn't teach me to pay attention to dull talk; it did the opposite

by providing plenty of strengthening practice for the ability to escape mentally. It was a survival technique in school, but a detriment in the real world. And it took years to break the habit.

Comment: Thinking about it . . . it's kind of funny. right now im sitting in school, being bored outta my head, i surf the internet, and i find this whole thing, i keep reading what the person wrote and what the reader wrote . . . and the whole class is finished now, and this whole thing kept me entertained . . . ya we do suffer from bordness . . . i dont think there is gonna be a solution . . . thats just nature . . . unless u find somethin to do . . .

Comment: Almost any teen in any school could be writing this today. Waiting for the next bell. Most of what goes on in school is so scheduled and programmed right down to the minute-by-minute detail of each lesson plan that it is almost more productive to color squares by the minute. Since children are so often bored in scheduled classes and don't pay attention, homework is assigned. Homework is documented evidence that school does not work like it is supposed to, for can any of us imagine spending almost eight hours a day in class and still needing to do "homework" to learn the lesson?

Pair these colorful excerpts with research findings from the 2007 & 2008 High School Survey of Student Engagement. This research project "conceives of student engagement as a deeper and broader construct, one that allows us to capture a variety of ways in which students may or may not be engaged in the life and work of a school" (Yazzie-Mintz, 2009, p. 2). The data in Figure 1.1 are excerpted from the extensive study of more than 134,000 student responses from a diverse representation of public high schools (91 percent of total sample) across the United States.

Educators and parents may bemoan the lack of self-discipline of today's learners, but it is unreasonable to expect children to commit themselves to work that is educationally deadening. Boredom not only weakens students' focus on their schoolwork, it can also engender frustration that can manifest itself in depression and anger. The following quote comes from Fritz Redl (1972), who has been described as the father of modern psychoeducation:

Boredom will always remain the greatest enemy of school discipline. If we remember that children are bored, not only when they don't happen to be interested in the subject or when the teacher doesn't make it interesting, but also when certain working conditions are out of focus with their basic needs, then we can realize what a great contributor to discipline problems boredom really is. Research has shown that boredom is closely related ✓ to frustration and that the effect of too much frustration is invariably irritability, withdrawal, rebellious opposition or aggressive rejection of the whole show. (297)

Figure 1.1	Data from the 2007 and 2008 High School Survey of Student Engagement

Pervasiveness of Boredom in School

- Two out of three respondents (67% in each year) are bored at least every day in class in high school.
- Approximately half of the students (51% in 2007, 50% in 2008) are bored every day.
- Approximately one out of every six students (16% in 2007, 17% in 2008) are bored in every class.
- Only 2% in each year report never being bored.

Reasons Why School Is Boring

- More than four out of five cited a reason for their boredom as "Material wasn't interesting" (83% in 2007, 82% in 2008).
- About two out of five students (41% in each year) claimed that the lack of relevance of the material caused their boredom.
- About one-third of the students (33% in 2007, 32% in 2008) were bored because "Work wasn't challenging enough."
- Just over one-fourth (27% in each year) of respondents were bored because "Work was too difficult."
- More than one-third of respondents (35% in each year) were bored due to "No interaction with teacher."

Perceived Impact of School on Future Success

Not more than one-third of the students reported that their school contributed "Very Much" to their growth in the following areas related to rigor and relevance:

- "Acquiring skills related to work after high school" (23% in 2007, 24% in 2008)
- "Writing effectively" (31% in 2007, 30% in 2008)
- "Speaking effectively" (27% in each year)
- "Thinking critically" (32% in each year)
- "Reading and understanding challenging materials" (28% in each year)
- "Learning independently" (28% in 2007, 30% in 2008)
- "Solving real-world problems" (20% in 2007, 21% in 2008)

Source: Adapted from Yazzie-Mintz, E. (2009). *Engaging the voices of students: A report on the 2007 and 2008 high school survey of student engagement* (pp. 5–8). Bloomington, IN: Center for Evaluation and Education Policy, Indiana University. Retrieved July 13, 2010, from http://indiana.edu/nceep/hssse/images/hssse_2009_report.pdf

Not surprisingly, many educators have become committed to the notion that improving student engagement is central to school effectiveness. In fact, when I was working with a group of administrators at a leadership retreat, it was the most commonly cited focus of site-based improvement plans. While the leaders believed that student boredom was a serious problem in elementary through high school, they were less clear on the source of that boredom. They had identified possible solutions (cooperative learning, technology tools, and performance tasks), but they were largely fixated on creating external sources of stimulation rather than examining the internal motivation of the learner. Boredom cannot be cured with neat tools and temporary breaks from drudgery; it is symptomatic of the profound disconnect between the learner and the learning organization. To blame, punish, or negatively label the learner for that disconnect is, at the very least, shortsighted. There is nothing wrong with our students as learners; they just don't learn well under the conditions we have designed.

Perhaps you are unmoved by how students "feel" about their learning experience. Some critics would in fact suggest that feelings are irrelevant; ultimately, school is about getting results and accomplishing targeted goals. Consider the following student achievement statistics for elementary, middle, and high school performance.

- Elementary and Middle School Performance

    – Just under one-third of American 4th and 8th graders show solid academic proficiency in reading and math. Proficiency represents demonstrated competency, application in real-world situations, and relevant analytical skills (National Assessment of Educational Progress, 2004a, 2004b).

    – On international comparisons in math, American 4th graders scored lower than 11 other countries and American 8th graders scored lower than 14 other countries (Mullis, Martin, & Foy, 2005).

- High School Performance

    – Despite an increase in college preparatory courses from 10 percent in 1982 to just over 50 percent in 2004, reading scores did not change and math scores only increased slightly (*NAEP Data Explorer*, 2010).

– On average, U.S. students scored lower than OECD average on the combined science and literacy scale (489 vs. 500) and mathematics scale (474 vs. 498) (U.S. Department of Education, National Center for Education Statistics, n.d.).

– In 1982, approximately 42 percent of high school students were on an academic track and 23 percent were on a vocational track; by 1998, 71 percent of students were on an academic track and only 4 percent were on a vocational track (Hoxby, 2003).

– The dropout rate is not necessarily a low-income issue; middle-income students made up 61.1 percent of dropouts from grades 10–12 in 2000 (Kaufman, Alt, & Chapman, 2001).

Some would suggest that school is designed not around the natural intelligence of the learner or around standardized test measures but rather around the knowledge that students must acquire in order to do well in college. They might say that boredom may be inevitable, but it's acceptable as long as those students who do graduate from high school have the appropriate knowledge base to continue their studies and assume more control of their course selection and future vocation. So how do students fare once they arrive at college?

- Postsecondary Education

  – College instructors estimate that 42 percent of college students are not adequately prepared for the demands of college by the education they received in high school; 39 percent of recent high school graduates enrolled in college say there are gaps in their preparation (Peter D. Hart Research Associates, 2005).

  – An ever-increasing proportion of high school students in the United States today aspire to college. Yet statistics indicate that the percentage of college students receiving bachelor's degrees has remained relatively constant over the past 25 years (Conley, 2005, p. xi).

– Somewhere between 30 and 60 percent of postsecondary students now require remedial education upon entry to college, depending on the type of institution they attend (Conley, 2005, p. xi).

David Conley posits that student struggles in subjects in science, technology, and mathematics originate in the lack of curricular alignment between high school and college, as well as inadequate development of students' cognitive, interpersonal, and study skills:

> Although many high schools do strive to challenge students to engage at deeper levels, the structure of the curriculum and the emphasis on simply completing required courses creates the wrong mentality. Students enter college expecting assignments and tests with clear right and wrong answers that do not require much interpretation or even much thinking. When interpretation is required, they often assume that any kind of interpretation will be acceptable and are surprised and even offended when they are told that they must apply certain disciplinary rules of thinking and analysis in order for their argument to be considered worthwhile or correct. In other words, they have completed the introduction to the discipline without developing the habits of mind necessary to engage fully in the study and understanding of that discipline. (Conley, 2005, pp. 75–76)

So let's review. Students begin their formal schooling as naturally intelligent, curious, joyful learners. Over time, they become joyless, bored learners who survive their K–12 education in order to acquire a high school diploma. If the unexciting realities of elementary and secondary education must be endured by students because of their youth and inexperience, then they should at least benefit in their postsecondary academic performance. But while 90 percent of students self-report their aspirations to attend college (Yazzie-Mintz, 2009), the number of students earning a college diploma has not increased, and the number of students who need remediation in their first years of college has increased dramatically. Given the boredom of students, mediocre results from our schools, and increasing concerns about students' ability to do college-level work, it becomes clear that the current design of schooling depresses the thinking, feeling, and achieving of too many of our learners.

Revisiting the Reflection Question

Is fundamental change possible given the myths about schooling?

Conclusion

This reflection question is intended to trigger not self-loathing or self-defense mechanisms, but rather true curiosity. For now, take comfort in the neurological truth that doing what we have always done is a familiar route that is not easily changed, due to the design of the brain and fear of the unknown. From the perspective of neuroscientist Richard Burton:

> The concept of neural networks also helps explain why established habits, beliefs, and judgments are so difficult to change. Imagine the gradual formation of a riverbed. The initial flow of water might be completely random—there are no preferred routes in the beginning. But once a creek has been formed, water is more likely to follow this newly created path of least resistance. As the water continues, the creek deepens and a river develops. . . . The brain is only human; it relies on established ways. As interneuronal connections increase, they become more difficult to overcome. (Burton, 2008, p. 52)

The discussion of the nine myths above calls attention to those ways of thinking that may be familiar, but still jeopardize the power and joy of learning for teacher and student alike. Change your thinking; change your experience. Chapter 2 delves more deeply into our "paths of least resistance" through the exploration of two additional (and more contemporary) problems: how economic changes have created new expectations for employability, and how multitasking has diluted the quality of focus and attention invested in all efforts.

Those readers worried about having to endure more discussion of problems should remember that the intent is to make the status quo no longer a comfortable place to reside. If the pain of analyzing the accepted realities of today's schools becomes palpable and excruciating—if the failures to successfully educate our students become undeniable—you will be free to imagine a better way. Chapter 6 will revisit the original nine myths with an idea-gathering and solution-finding perspective through the sharing of strategies, processes, and exemplars.

Conceptual Frame

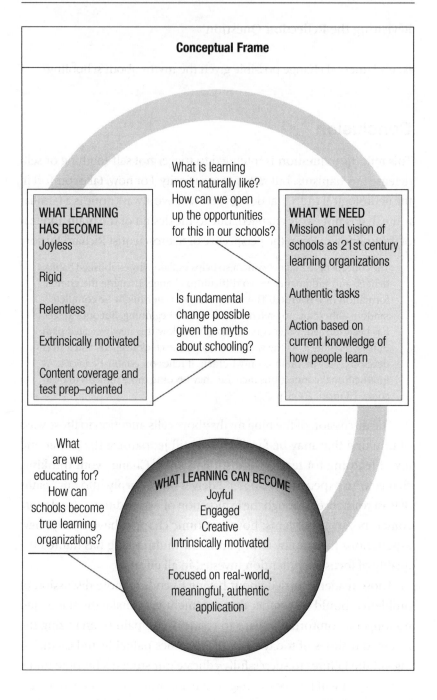

What is learning most naturally like? How can we open up the opportunities for this in our schools?

WHAT LEARNING HAS BECOME
Joyless

Rigid

Relentless

Extrinsically motivated

Content coverage and test prep–oriented

Is fundamental change possible given the myths about schooling?

WHAT WE NEED
Mission and vision of schools as 21st century learning organizations

Authentic tasks

Action based on current knowledge of how people learn

What are we educating for? How can schools become true learning organizations?

WHAT LEARNING CAN BECOME
Joyful
Engaged
Creative
Intrinsically motivated

Focused on real-world, meaningful, authentic application

2

The Illusion of Accomplishment

There is no denying the amount of work dedicated teachers and administrators put into making schools better, but all that effort merely gives off the illusion of accomplishment. Despite school improvement plans, accountability controls, and investment in technology tools, the way schools are designed today fails to prepare students for the world that awaits them after graduation day. Three core problems hinder the effectiveness of our schools. The first problem, students' feelings of disconnection from their schoolwork, was discussed in depth in Chapter 1. This chapter delves deeply into two additional problems that have more contemporary origins:

- The demands on the 21st century worker and citizen have shifted, affecting the way students are expected to think, work, and interact with others, yet the classroom remains teacher-directed and highly routinized.
- The way time is organized in school and outside of school, with a never-ending list of assignments to accomplish, has made deep learning less possible.

While there are certainly other factors at play (standardized testing, federal and state policy, freedom and tyranny of local control), I have deliberately chosen to focus only on those factors which you, the reader, can change by opening up "space" in your own mind first, and then extending that to improve the quality of thinking and experience for the students in your classroom and school.

Candidly discussing these problems will help us to begin to let go of old habits and routines that no longer serve our students well. Whether you are motivated by the need for students to become gainfully employed or by the need to restore joy to learning, know this: we can improve the quality of learning immediately. It starts with slowing down the pace of our thinking, refusing to jump to conclusions, and introducing discomfort with the pervasive weariness that characterizes too many experiences in our schools.

Lack of Preparation for the 21st Century Workplace

For several decades now, leaders in politics, business, and education have pressed schools to better prepare students for a 21st century world. Such a transformation requires rethinking every aspect of the "game of school," because the game of life has changed. The initial demands to renovate the schoolhouse were based on the theoretical notion that one day, the world would be different and the competitive advantage would go to those nations that trained their workforce to adapt to those realities. Then something peculiar happened—the 21st century showed up, and the world changed, yet the conversations about 21st century schools remain largely theoretical.

In an industry-based economy, there were basic expectations about the employer-employee relationship. There was a clear hierarchy of roles and responsibilities, and workers respected the chain of command. Employees who followed company rules and did good work had the potential to move up in the organization. Seniority mattered—young employees were expected to "put in their time" in order to receive increased status and influence. Employees remained with one company for long periods; it was considered normal for employees to be "lifers" within an organization, providing stability for both employer and employee alike.

In modern times, the nature of work has fundamentally changed. The workplace that students will enter features the following characteristics:

- Global interdependence
- Rapid exchange of information and ideas
- Increased pressure for fiscal transparency
- Constant pursuit of innovation
- Personal and professional relationships conducted largely through electronic correspondence (and sometimes through virtual or game-based worlds)
- Economic and social responsibility for more sustainable practices
- Renewed appreciation of creativity

Organizations have become "flatter" as employees at all levels are expected to think, collaborate, and problem solve without depending upon their superiors for answers. Even young employees can become part of the leadership team (or run the corporation). Job security is tenuous as job descriptions, markets, and technologies continue to change. There is less permanence, certainty, and stability than ever before, but at the same time, there is more opportunity for creativity, innovation, flexibility, and personalization. There are also notable shifts in demographics of the workforce:

- Over half (57 percent) of U.S. CEOs report education and workforce preparedness is a "very important" or "most important" policy issue. Nearly three-quarters (73 percent) of those CEOs who report having difficulty finding qualified workers in the United States rate global competitiveness as "very important" or "most important."
- Between 2000 and 2010, the number of workers ages 35–44 decreased by 10 percent, and those ages 16–24 increased by 15 percent.
- Between 2000 and 2015, about 85 percent of newly created U.S. jobs will require education beyond high school. (The Conference Board, The Partnership for 21st Century Skills, 2006)

These changes place even more pressure on both K–12 and postsecondary schools to educate students in ways that will enable them to meet new challenges, responsibilities, and opportunities successfully.

So how are our students doing, according to the business leaders who hire them? Not very well. The "Workforce Readiness Report Card for New Entrants to the Workforce" (The Conference Board et al., 2006; see Figure 2.1) was compiled through data collected from 431 employers "representing a combined workforce of over 2 million U.S. based employees" (The Conference Board et al., 2006, p. 60). While workforce readiness is the responsibility of postsecondary education programs as well, 75.6 percent of survey respondents hold K–12 schools responsible for providing the knowledge and skills necessary for new workers to be successful. The dissatisfaction of employers, the rising need for remediation among students entering college (discussed previously), and the unimpressive achievement of our students compared with those in other nations (Mullis et al., 2005; National Assessment of Educational Progress, 2004a, 2004b) combine to illuminate a deeply rooted problem. Labeling this situation a crisis stirs up emotion and generates headlines, but it does little to address the fundamental issue: we may be well-intentioned and dedicated to the children we serve, but we are not getting the job done.

Reflection Question

If the world has changed in profound ways, what effect should those changes have on the mission of our schools?

Cultural Change Must Lead to Educational Change

Substantive changes in the economy, the perceived value of a high school diploma, the demographics of our population, and the expectations of what prospective employees know and are able to do—all of

Figure 2.1	Workforce Readiness Report Card for New Entrants to Workforce

Workforce Readiness Report Card for New Entrants to Workforce

Assessment of new workforce entrant readiness on "very important" skills (basic knowledge and applied skills rated as "very important" by a majority of employer respondents). "Very important" skills are placed on the Deficiency/Excellence lists if at least 1 in 5 respondents report entrant readiness as "deficient" or "excellent."

High School Students

Deficiency	Excellence
Written Communications 80.9%	No skills are on the Excellence list for new
Professionalism/Work Ethic 70.3%	entrants with a high school diploma.
Critical Thinking/Problem Solving 69.6%	
Oral Communications 52.7%	
Ethics/Social Responsibility 44.1%	
Reading Comprehension 38.4%	
Teamwork/Collaboration 34.6%	
Diversity 27.9%	
Information Technology Application. 21.5%	
English Language 21.0%	

Source: The Conference Board, The Partnership for 21st Century Skills, Corporate Voices for Working Families, & The Society for Human Resource Management. (2006). *Are they really ready to work? Employers' perspectives on the basic knowledge and applied skills of new entrants to the 21st century U.S. workforce* (p. 41). Tucson, AZ: The Partnership for 21st Century Skills. © 2006 by The Conference Board, Inc., The Partnership for 21st Century Skills, Corporate Voices for Working Families, & The Society for Human Resource Management. Reprinted by permission.

these factors should have significant impact on what we teach and the way we teach it. For over a century, because of the long-standing belief in authority of the teacher and the power of the high school diploma, teaching pedagogy based on lecture, rote learning, and memorization was accepted as appropriate. These teacher-centered learning environments were designed to impart knowledge and skills so that students were prepared to execute procedures, demonstrate a strong work ethic, and follow the established chain of command. K–12 schools were representative of other large institutions that valued efficiency, clear protocols, and stability. The teacher's job was to teach; the student's job was to learn. Schools were not expected to teach all children to reach the same levels, and those who were college-bound were given different instructional programs from the ones given to those who would instead enter the workplace.

Enacting the kind of change needed to foster more adaptive learning environments (ones that incorporate flexible, multidisciplinary, technology-rich ways for students to collaborate, problem solve, create, and communicate) will require a fundamental disruption of the status quo, an inherently difficult process. Educators must revisit the mission of schooling in more substantive ways than simply adding the words "in a 21st century world" to the end of a decade(s)-old statement. Tony Wagner speaks to the magnitude of this task:

> Teaching all students to think and to be curious is much more than a technical problem for which educators, alone, are accountable. And more professional development for teachers and better textbooks and tests, though necessary, are insufficient as solutions. The problem goes much deeper—to the very way we conceive of the purpose and experience of schooling and what we expect our high school graduates to know and be able to do. (Quoted in Partnership for 21st Century Skills, 2008, p. 11)

While there have been multiple recent attempts to reform instructional policy to make it more responsive to students (e.g., differentiated instruction, integration of technology, project-based learning), the dynamic of the classroom has largely remained tightly controlled by the teacher. Industry leaders know all too well how difficult it is to stay innovative once a viable business model has been created. The bold ideas, strategies, and products that inspire a company's initial success become more mainstream as leaders spend more time refining existing processes than exploring new alternatives. When new ideas do emerge, they are often tweaked beyond recognition to minimize the impact on the organization.

This predictable institutional behavior has been particularly evident and disheartening in schools during the past decade, even as education leaders push for the inclusion of 21st century skills. I have heard on multiple occasions from teachers that these skills are merely "what we've always done" with a new spin. If we tweak the requirement to teach the 21st century skills of critical thinking and problem solving to justify the assignment of two dozen single-path, single-solution math problems, or relegate creative and agile thinking to what students do when they have finished their required assignments or during extracurricular time, then we haven't even begun to enter the modern era.

Addressing the following six needs of 21st century schooling will provide the guidance we need to create more naturally powerful learning organizations:

- Learning goals need to address both applied and basic skills
- Students need to employ creative and innovative thinking
- Students need to work at meaningful tasks
- Students need to become lifelong learners
- Students need to maximize their personal health and wellness
- Parents need to hold schools accountable

Learning Goals Need to Address Both Applied and Basic Skills

The skills that students need to be competitive have been defined by several national organizations, most notably by The Partnership for 21st Century Skills (2008). Listed below are six key areas that this Partnership believes are crucial to our learners' future success:

- **Thinking critically and making judgments** about the barrage of information that comes their way every day—on the Web, in the media, in homes, workplaces and everywhere else. . . .

- **Solving complex, multidisciplinary, open-ended problems** that all workers, in every kind of workplace, encounter routinely. . . . Businesses expect employees at all levels to identify problems, think through solutions and alternatives, and explore new options if their approaches don't pan out. . . .

- **Creativity and entrepreneurial thinking**—a skill set highly associated with job creation. . . . Many of the fastest-growing jobs and emerging industries rely on workers' creative capacity—the ability to think unconventionally, question the herd, imagine new scenarios, and produce astonishing work. . . .

- **Communicating and collaborating** with teams of people across cultural, geographic and language boundaries—a necessity in diverse and multinational workplaces and communities. . . .

- **Making innovative use of knowledge, information and opportunities** to create new services, processes and products. The global marketplace rewards organizations that rapidly and routinely find better ways of doing things. . . .

• **Taking charge of financial, health and civic responsibilities** and making wise choices. From deciding how to invest their savings to choosing a health care plan, Americans need more specialized skills—simply because the options are increasingly complex and the consequences of poor decisions could be dire. (p. 10)

While the work of this organization and others to define the skills most vital for future success has been invaluable, the real dilemma is how to meaningfully incorporate these skills into school curricula. Most educators agree that current curricular documents are already overloaded with more goals, tasks, and activities than time available. Given that fact, it is absolutely unreasonable to hand a new list of skills to teaching staff and ask them to use it in their classroom-level practice, especially if they are simultaneously expected to make low-level test prep a priority. (It is only fair to note, however, that many state assessments have become quite sophisticated in their design and do require the higher-level thinking captured by some of the above 21st century skills.) This need to address applied skills cannot be layered on top of what we currently expect all students to know, be able to do, and understand; it requires a serious reevaluation of all curriculum goals and instructional practices from the ground up in order to create the necessary space for learners to engage in this more rigorous critical thinking and problem solving. Chapter 3 will illustrate how the meaningful incorporation of 21st century skills can be achieved at the systems level through the development of new mission and vision statements; Chapter 4 will address designing tasks to measure those goals.

Students Need to Employ Creative and Innovative Thinking

While creativity is just one of the defined 21st century skills, it is the one most frequently dismissed, misunderstood, and marginalized in school curricula. Nevertheless, creativity has become significantly important to business leaders and increasingly prominent in our national conversations. (Consider, for example, the popularity of Daniel Pink's *A Whole New Mind*, 2005.) Richard Florida (2004) chronicles the shift in the skill set of the workforce away from one centered on data analysis, efficiency, and predictability to one encompassing creativity, autonomy, and personal identity:

> Many say that we now live in an "information" economy or a "knowledge" economy. But what's more fundamentally true is that we now have an economy powered by human creativity. Creativity—"the ability to create meaningful new forms," as Webster's dictionary puts it—is now the decisive source of competitive advantage. (pp. 4–5)

The push to continuously improve ourselves and our lives has ushered in new technologies as well as new industries that make it increasingly possible to break down the conventional boundaries regulating how people think, work, play, and communicate.

Not only is creativity vital to the economic viability of our workforce, but it is also important in extending our learners' capacity to wonder, to explore the unknown, to think of entrenched problems from a new perspective, and to experience the joy of producing original thought. A more substantive conversation about the creative process and how to embed it in instructional practice will take place in Chapter 4. For now, this need is an important reminder that it is a learning goal, not a luxury, to develop the imaginations of our students as they work to solve problems, produce texts, and develop new ideas.

Students Need to Work at Meaningful Tasks

The assignments students are given largely focus on foundational knowledge and skills at the expense of inquiry, deep knowledge, flexible applications, and alternate points of view. While many teachers profess that they are limited in their abilities to design more meaningful tasks because of rigid pacing guides and standardized testing, it is curious that more progress hasn't been made. If we know that the work we give students should be designed to prepare them for postsecondary success, shouldn't the assignments that students complete correspond with what employers and professors value? A report examining the way employers view the way colleges prepare students for the workplace (Peter D. Hart Research Associates, 2008) states:

> When it comes to the assessment practices that employers trust to indicate a graduate's level of knowledge and potential to succeed in the job world,

employers dismiss tests of general content knowledge in favor of assessments of real-world and applied-learning approaches. Multiple-choice tests specifically are seen as ineffective. On the other hand, assessments that employers hold in high regard include evaluations of supervised internships, community-based projects, and comprehensive senior projects. (p. 1)

Many educators have informed me that it is unreasonable to expect such fundamental changes when standardized testing evaluates students in a less sophisticated manner. In recent years, many states have begun to improve standardized tests to include more authentic problem-solving and critical-thinking tasks. These changes have actually made it increasingly difficult to "teach to the test," because the test items focus more on application of knowledge, critical thinking, and analysis than on comprehension and skill demonstrations. Let's face it: it is easier for teachers to design, administer, and score more straightforward assessments of knowledge and skills. It is also easier for students to study for those examinations and for students and parents to understand the results. But meaningful tasks do more than just measure student learning—they also motivate the learner. When the work provides students with a goal that they can pursue, a purpose for why they are doing what they are doing, and a tangible benefit to individuals outside of the classroom, students are more likely to experience the flow that comes with deep engagement. Not only do they learn how to make sense of the new, the unfamiliar, and the seemingly impossible, they also build powerful conceptual connections that make knowledge and skills stick in their long-term memory. This subject will be discussed more fully in Chapter 4, which explores assessments designed to provide students with meaningful opportunities to demonstrate their learning in authentic contexts.

Students Need to Become Lifelong Learners

Because of the need to be able to approach problems from a fresh perspective and navigate change, the modern worker must become a lifelong learner. While many school mission statements have espoused this abstract goal for years, it has become imperative to employability. In *Are They Really Ready to Work?* (The Conference Board et al., 2006) and *The Global Achievement Gap* (Wagner, 2008), business leaders describe the importance of lifelong learning to an individual's (and a company's) long-term success:

> *Stephen Wing, Director of Government Programs at CVS:* Lifelong learning is a critical connection people need to continue to pursue. People may have five or six jobs during their employment. In fact, in an increasingly knowledge-based economy, where the need is for flexible knowledge and skills and the ability to move easily from one job to another, the number of careers in a professional lifetime may be as many as 10 to 14. (The Conference Board et al., 2006, p. 37)

> *Clay Parker, President of the Chemical Management Division of BOC Edwards:* [An employee at BOC Edwards] has to think, be flexible, change, and be adaptive and use a variety of tools to solve new problems. We change what we do all the time. I've been here four years, and we've done fundamental reorganization every year because of changes in the business. People have to learn to adapt. I can guarantee that the job I hire someone to do will change or may not exist in the future, so this is why adaptability and learning skills are more important than technical skills. (Wagner, 2008, p. 30)

> *Karen Bruett, manager of strategic business development in K–12 education at Dell and past president of the Partnership for 21st Century Skills:* People's jobs change very rapidly. I've been at Dell a long time in similar sales and marketing functions—but what I do today versus what I did five or six years ago is completely different. To survive, you have to be flexible and adaptable and a lifelong learner. . . . And so some of the key competencies we hold employees accountable for include the ability to deal with ambiguity, the ability to learn on the fly, and strategic agility. . . . What goes on in classrooms today is the same stuff as fifty years ago, and that's just not going to cut it. (Wagner, 2008, pp. 30–31)

Lifelong learning affects employees' viability both with their current employer and in the future careers they will pursue. There is no guarantee that the job you are doing today and the people you are doing it with will be the same six weeks, six months, or six years from now. Members of the workforce, regardless of their job title or occupation, are expected to continually adapt and change.

An important side note: one of the few professions that have remained relatively stable is that of classroom teacher. While the pressures and initiatives have increased in recent years, the basic job description is the same: teachers spend virtually all of their professional day teaching an assigned set of students an assigned curriculum. Although major changes may have been proposed in their respective schools, few of those efforts have significantly affected daily practices within and across classrooms. If our students are to become lifelong learners, we must model lifelong learning in our own work as educators. We need to grow and experiment with a plethora of ideas in order to reinvigorate our professional imaginations and engagement in the work. We need to push the boundaries of our thinking about how to structure learning so that it is more powerful, accessible, and fruitful for all learners. As a profession, we must collectively practice what we preach. This conversation will continue in Chapter 3 with discussion of how to renovate the 21st century schoolhouse.

Students Need to Maximize Their Personal Health and Wellness

While an individual worker in the 21st century has more opportunity to do self-directed, personally meaningful work than ever before, there is also greater instability, stress, and intolerance for investing necessary resources. Richard Florida (2004) describes the impact this stress has on the worker:

> Not all is rosy in this emerging mainstream of the Creative Age. With no big company to provide security, we bear much more risk than the corporate and working classes of the organizational age did. We experience and often create high levels of mental and emotional stress, at work and at home. We crave flexibility but have less time to pursue the things we truly desire. The technologies that were supposed to liberate us from work have invaded our lives. (pp. 10–11)

In fact, the "emerging content area deemed most critical" to survey respondents in *Are They Really Ready to Work?* (The Conference Board et al., 2006) was the area of personal health and wellness; 76.1 percent of respondents indicated that this area is "most critical for future graduates" (p. 52). Not only is health and wellness a concern for the adults, but it has also dominated conversations about our children. We openly worry about the negative impacts of homework assignments, length of the school day, lack of physical fitness, increased substance abuse (legal and illegal), and poor nutrition. Few schools, however, make it a priority to teach the skills necessary to improve health and wellness. Look at the current design of—and instructional minutes devoted to—physical and health education in your school. Look at the current foods available in the cafeteria and the current policies about eating in the school. Look at the current curricular role that guidance counselors, social workers, and school psychologists have in promoting social and emotional health for the full student body. It is difficult to teach what we do not live in our daily lives. Students observe how their teachers, administrators, and parents struggle to manage their lives and find ways to cope with stress (some ways more healthy than others). This issue will be addressed further in the section on our relationship with time.

Parents Need to Hold Schools Accountable

Parents consistently rate their children's schools highly, even though the general public has a less favorable impression. Nationwide, 26 percent of Americans would give public schools a grade of A or B. However, 61 percent of parents give the schools in their own community an A or B (Rose & Gallup, 2004). Following are more statistics that show a disturbing trend:

- In 1973, 58 percent of Americans said they had "a great deal" or "quite a lot" of confidence in the public schools. Ten years later, in 1983, this figure dropped to 39 percent; it fell a little further to 36 percent in 1999. By 2003, it had only increased to 40 percent (Report Card on America's Schools, n.d.).

- The public expects change in the public schools to come through reform, not alternative solutions. Given the choice, 66 percent of the public chose to reform the existing system, while only 26 percent opted for seeking an alternative to the status quo (Rose & Gallup, 2004).

- The public believes that the quality of a student's teacher is the most important factor in determining student achievement (45 percent), ahead of parental involvement (29 percent), facilities and resources (12 percent), or the quality of the principal (3 percent) (Report Card on America's Schools, n.d.).

- More than 80 percent of Americans say the push to raise academic standards is a "move in the right direction," and nearly half of parents (47 percent) say the standards in their state are not tough enough (Report Card on America's Schools, n.d.).

How do we make sense of these findings? Why aren't parents harder on their children's schools? I personally experienced this conundrum during one of my consulting projects. The leadership team in one school district wanted to rethink its work from top to bottom to create an educational experience that was more meaningful and relevant to the 21st century learner. We conducted a series of focus groups for parents, board members, and civic leaders to allow them to share their thoughts and perceptions about the role of schooling in the 21st century so that school leaders could develop an effective long-range plan to ensure current and future success for students. Our rationale was that if parents and community members could articulate the profound differences in the world outside of school, they too would give voice to the need for profound differences within school. Listed below were the questions used to frame the conversation:

1. What was your school experience like?
    a. Structure—how school was organized
    b. Classroom environment—role of teacher, key routines, primary instructional tools
    c. Purpose—preparation for the "outside world"
2. What are the most significant changes to the "outside world" since you were in school?
3. What has your child's/children's school experience been like?
    a. Structure—how school was organized
    b. Classroom environment—role of teacher, key routines, primary instructional tools
    c. Purpose—preparation for the "outside world"
4. The following five key competencies are the hallmarks of a 21st century school. For each one, what do you think it means? Why do you think it matters?
    a. Critical thinking and problem solving
    b. Imaginative, agile, innovative thinking
    c. Collaboration
    d. Effective communication
    e. Personal meaning
5. What kind of experiences should our students have to prepare them for the 21st century world?

It was fascinating to listen to just how different school life was "back in the day" for the parents, grandparents, and great-grandparents of today's generation of students. Participants spoke at great length and detail about their own childhood challenges, classroom experiences, and favorite memories of teachers. They also were quite articulate and passionate about how much the workplace has changed since they first entered it several years (or several decades) ago.

Even more fascinating, however, was their hesitancy or unwillingness to question the appropriateness of their own children's educational experience in light of this conversation. On an abstract level, they assumed that the work in schools provided their children with a solid foundation for postsecondary success. Yet they also openly acknowledged that if you took the technology tools away, much of what happened in their children's classroom was very similar to what happened in their own. Whether out of respect, reluctance, or ignorance, not one member of any of the focus groups aggressively pursued the obvious question: "If the world has changed so much, why haven't schools changed along with it?"

Upon revisiting this question several months later, I garnered some insight as to why parents are reluctant to question the relevance of schooling as it stands today. As a parent of two elementary-school-age children myself, I realized that I ask the following of their education:

- I want my children to be happy at school.
- I want them to feel connected to their teacher.
- I want them to come home and be able to tell me something interesting that they learned that day.
- I want them to do their best and feel proud of their accomplishments.
- I want them to receive feedback on their work that they can use to improve it.
- I want them to be more knowledgeable, skillful, and strategic as a result of their work.

Looking through the lens of my own experience, the incongruous data began to make sense. When my children have a great teacher, all is right with the world. When my children have a weak teacher, I am concerned about the individual, not the system. We focus more on the relationship between teacher and child and the communication of success or failure than on amorphous considerations about the larger aims of schooling and whether ours and other people's children are faring well in the long term. It is easier to consider the relatively more tangible issue of the effectiveness of the teacher than it is to question the effectiveness of the system.

The question "Is my child doing well at school?" could be turned on its head: "Is school doing well by my child?" Parents of children with special needs have long lobbied systems to become more responsive to their learners. What if all parents did the same? What if they demanded that their children be given more interesting work to do? More inspiring texts to read? More complex problems to solve? More tools to express their ideas? More opportunities to showcase their work? Parents know their children, they know what life in a 21st century workplace requires, and they know what they see come home in their children's backpacks. If parents began to demand something more, it would provide us with a much-needed push in the right direction. Not only would it create additional urgency to do better by our students, but it would also dispel the often-cited reason that change isn't possible: parents won't like it.

Educators often claim that changes in assessment, grading, and instructional practices that put more emphasis on authentic learning, grading for achievement, and differentiated instruction are not well received by parents. Some responses to the prospect of change include the following:

- "Parents want to see lots of grades in my grade book, so I have to generate a lot of small quizzes and tests."
- "Parents don't like it when students are given tasks or problems with no right answer because they don't get how its graded or how to help their child do well."
- "Parents want their child to get the same treatment as every other child—differentiated instruction seems unfair to them."

- "Parents just want their children to get good grades, and that means if their kids are currently successful, they don't want the rules to change."
- "Parents think that rigor means that kids have to get a lot of homework, so I give them what they expect."

While there are a number of parents who express these or similar sentiments to educators, it is important to note that they, too, have been trained by the system to play by its rules in order to maximize their children's opportunity for success. Including them in the larger conversations contained in this book enables them to become partners in our concern for the well-being of our students, both in the present and future, as well as partners in the innovation of schooling. We need their expertise about their own child/children and their experience in their respective careers to strengthen the relevance and significance of learning for all.

Before we move into the final section of this chapter, it is important to pause to allow the discussion about 21st century realities to sink in. Any reader who has spent much of his or her professional life working in schools may need more time to explore these needs further. I have found that classroom teachers struggle to accept that 21st century skills are different from current practices. There are powerful books on just this subject for those of you who want to do more reading. (Tony Wagner's *The Global Achievement Gap* [2008] is a personal favorite.)

Revisiting the Reflection Question

If the world has changed in profound ways, what impact should those changes have on the mission of our schools?

- Reflect on how the world has changed within the scope of your own lifetime.
- Reflect on what you believe the next generation of learners will need in order to live productive, fulfilling lives so that they have the power to achieve their goals and contribute to the well-being of others.

- Reflect on one new dimension that you can make an integral part of your work in/with schools to help students achieve this new goal.
- Reflect on one existing practice or policy that you may be able to eliminate.

Rethinking Our Relationship to Time

At the heart of this discussion is how we think about and use the time we have to do our jobs—a common theme that comes up in both the nine myths from Chapter 1 and the six needs for 21st century schooling. Without question, time is in short supply in schools. Lack of time is often cited as the number-one obstacle to curriculum completion, staff conversations about student work and instructional planning on deep levels, and the opportunity for students to revise their work or pursue areas of personal interest. While it is true that time is tight, finding more time would not eliminate student discontent. In fact, few students are clamoring for a longer school day or school year; the time they already spend in school feels like an eternity to many.

Reflection Question

What does it feel like to be a learner in a classroom where time is always in short supply?

The stress caused by being chronically rushed engenders rigidity, bad feelings, and diminished performance for students and teachers. The relentless pace of so many curricular programs has everyone flying from one topic to another in an attempt to complete everything before time runs out. How can there be joy, genuine exploration, and passion for the discipline when there is constant pressure to "get it" and move on? Is it possible to make a commitment to a text, a problem situation, phenomena, social injustice, or possible innovation when the duration of the learning experience is of predetermined minimal duration?

Virtually all teachers report that they would like more time, but there is often little consensus about what they would do with that time that isn't possible under the current schedule. Educators will emphatically argue that their hands are tied—they are doing the best they can with the limited time they have and the mountain of learning goals to accomplish. You, perhaps, are thinking similar thoughts as you read this. But as certain as people may be that time is the problem, I would suggest considering the possibility that the primary culprit is not our lack of time, but how we experience it. Consider an analogy offered by Vietnamese Buddhist monk Thich Nhat Hanh (1975) about washing the dishes:

> If while washing the dishes, we think only of the cup of tea that awaits us, thus hurrying to get the dishes out of the way as if they were a nuisance, then we are not "washing the dishes to wash the dishes." What's more, we are not alive during the time we are washing the dishes. In fact we are completely incapable of realizing the miracle of life while standing at the sink. If we can't wash the dishes, the chances are we won't be able to drink our tea either. While drinking the cup of tea, we will only be thinking of other things, barely aware of the cup in our hands. Thus we are sucked away into the future—and we are incapable of actually living one minute of life. (pp. 4–5)

Apply this metaphor while reflecting on instructional practices in your classroom, school building, or district. When time is too hurried, assignments become items on a to-do list, with firm deadlines that must be met so that the next tasks can be completed. Tangents and curiosities are interesting, but they distract from the questions on the table already; revision of current work becomes less important than the production of work in the first place; and collaboration becomes a more efficient way of getting a task done instead of a time to slow down and entertain alternate perspectives. The constant sprint wears teachers and students down earlier and earlier in the school year, which affects their willingness to reflect on their work or to find the energy to improve their performance. The following quotations illustrate why many of us have become increasingly stressed about time:

> When we feel that we are investing attention in a task against our will, it is as if our psychic energy is being wasted. Instead of helping us reach our own goals, it is called upon to make someone else's come true. The

> time channeled into such a task is perceived as time subtracted from the total available for our life. Many people consider their jobs as something they have to do, a burden imposed from the outside, an effort that takes away from the ledger of their existence. So even [though] the momentary on-the-job experience may be positive, they tend to discount it because it does not contribute to their own long-range goals. (Csikszentmihalyi, 1990, p. 160)

> Even when we are not actually pressed for time, we may perceive that [we are] because our time is literally worth more than it used to be. . . . We assign an ever-increasing cost to every minute we spend outside work— and thus worry constantly about the minutes slipping away. (Florida, 2004, p. 151)

When the teacher's job in effect becomes management of the curriculum and the students, the ensuing work that results often is unsatisfying for all parties involved. There is no space for joy, wonderment, intrigue, fascination, or contemplation when there is no time to breathe.

The relentless pace within the classroom is mirrored in the world outside of school as well. More people are more harried than ever before. It is common to see people multitask in all areas of their lives— exercising while talking on a cell phone and reading a magazine, driving while eating and reading map directions, writing an e-mail while answering a phone call and adding an item to a to-do list, having a conversation with your children while planning dinner and thinking about what has to get done before bedtime. Multitasking has become a behavioral fixture of our lives, so much so that many take pride in their ability to get so many things done at once.

Reflection Questions

What if in our efforts to move faster we actually get further behind?

What if our aggressive pace actually weakens our performance and sense of happiness?

Recent research on multitasking has revealed that multitasking is a neurological illusion. The tasks that appear to be performed simultaneously are not truly simultaneous; instead, the brain must switch focus from one task to another, causing pressure that degrades the overall quality of the task performance. Hamilton (2008) quotes researcher David Meyer, who has been studying multitasking for several decades:

> "For tasks that are at all complicated, no matter how good you have become at multitasking, you're still going to suffer hits against your performance. You will be worse compared to if you were actually concentrating from start to finish on the task," Meyer says.
>
> Multitasking causes a kind of brownout in the brain. Meyer says all the lights go dim because there just isn't enough power to go around. So, the brain starts shutting things down—things like neural connections to important information. . . .
>
> The technical name for creating, or recreating, these neural pathways [while you learn] is "spreading activation." It involves building connections step by step. . . . When we're interrupted, re-establishing those connections can take seconds or hours. "It goes on subconsciously and eventually, if I'm lucky, I get back up to speed with what I was thinking about before," Meyer says. (paragraphs 13–15, 18, 20–21)

Russell Poldrack, the author of another study, states, "Multi-tasking adversely affects how you learn. . . .Even if you learn while multi-tasking, that learning is less flexible and more specialized, so you cannot retrieve the information as easily. Our study shows that to the degree you can learn while multi-tasking, you will use different brain systems" ("Multitasking Adversely Affects Brain's Learning," paragraph 2). The conclusions of these studies suggest that the depth and flexibility of learning are affected by focus during learning. When you pair the relentless pace to cover the curriculum and prepare for standardized tests with the illusion of productivity that multitasking brings, you get a recipe for chronic weariness and limited satisfaction for teacher and student alike.

Despite research findings in the areas of neuroscience and workplace productivity, many people are reluctant or unwilling to stop multitasking. For those of you who incessantly check your handheld devices, consider the following. Sebastian Rupley (2005) reported about a productivity study commissioned by Hewlett-Packard to determine the impact of "the constant barrage of e-mail, instant messages, and cell-phone calls." There are many ways to measure that, but a new study

from England found strong evidence that constant interruptions reduce
mental acuity:

> The study . . . focused on 1,100 Britons and was conducted by TNS
> Research. As part of the research, Dr. Glenn Wilson, a psychiatrist at King's
> College London University, tracked the IQ of workers throughout the
> day in 80 clinical trials. He found that the IQ of those who tried to juggle
> messages and work fell by 10 points—more than double the 4-point fall
> seen after smoking marijuana. (paragraph 2)

Maybe that finding strikes you as ridiculous or far-fetched. But upon
reporting this finding to administrators during a workshop, participants
often share with me that multitasking is a compulsion: "When the
e-mail sound 'dings,' I just have to look to make sure everything is okay."
Others have described it as a way to get more accomplished: "If I am sitting in a meeting where an agenda item (or the entire agenda) does not
directly involve me, isn't it more productive to work on something else?"
I would suggest that this is not a knowledge problem but a habitual
problem. We have trained ourselves to become highly distracted; therefore, we can retrain ourselves to become more mindful. Recent research
about the neuroplasticity of the brain reveals that people who meditate
regularly can change how their brain functions. Brain scientist Richard
Davidson used functional magnetic resonance imagery to confirm that
"compassion meditation, even in short-term practitioners, induced
significant changes in patterns of functional activity in the brain" (Ryan,
2009, paragraph 14).

Can we teach something that we don't practice to our children? A
friend of mine shared a possibly apocryphal story that crystallizes my
concern. A parent brought his child for a consultation with Mahatma
Gandhi for advice on how to get the child to stop eating so many sweets.
Upon hearing the concern, Gandhi asked for them to return in six
weeks' time. After six weeks, the parent returned and reported that there
had been no change. He inquired as to what should have transpired during that time. Gandhi reportedly said that he couldn't teach something
that he didn't know, so the six weeks were for Gandhi to experience what
it was like to give up sugar. We must first learn to slow down our thinking, become more mindful, and open ourselves up to the possibilities
of fresh thought before we can begin to expect it from others.

Mindfulness can be cultivated through structured opportunities (a class, workshop, or conference on meditation, or a mindfulness curriculum such as the one developed by the Hawn Foundation), but the real "training" comes from consistent practice and recognition that you are wired to be calm. Robin Charbit and Charlie Kiefer, co-founders of Insight Management Partners, offer sage advice about how to improve the quality of life by understanding the role of thought on their Web site, www.insightmanagementpartners.com. For some readers, mindfulness may be part of your existing knowledge base; for others, it may seem to be an odd tangent for a mainstream education book on school effectiveness to take. This is important territory, however, as we continue in our pursuit of a more creative learning organization that provides the space for deep thinking, exploration, and the development of new ideas.

Those who know me personally are probably chuckling to themselves as they read this section. I'm known for my fast-paced thinking and my relentless pursuit of task completion. But I am also known to periodically pause and ask the question, "Is this all there is?" Whenever I race against time, I find that I lose. I finish, but I miss the meaning. I'm exhausted, and I don't know whether my effort ultimately made a difference. Are you ever bone-tired at the end of the day, but unsure what you spent your time doing, whether it had any effect, and how you will find the energy to do it again tomorrow? That's the power of the "washing the dishes" metaphor for students and educators alike. When we inhabit an experience instead of worrying about or longing for what's coming up next, we have the opportunity to learn—to question, to reflect, to struggle, and to break through.

Conclusion

Many educators are stressed to the breaking point. One school leader said to me that she knew that there must be a better way of working but was afraid to "let go of current practices" for fear that she would "drown in the abyss of the unknown." This tight grip on the status quo endures even as dissatisfaction with student learning grows, leaving educators painfully trapped between an outdated model of education that no longer works and a new model of education that doesn't yet exist. The more thinly we stretch our current resources to preserve an outdated, unnatural way of learning, the more weary we all become.

While there have been numerous attempts to reform educational practices to make learning more meaningful and rigorous for students, most have resulted only in short-lived improvement initiatives that have done little to change the instructional core in our schools. The constant search for the "next big thing" that will drive school improvement continues to take leaders further away from the true source of the problem. School staff need to look inward to restore the relationship between the learners and the learning organization. This requires a fundamental shift away from a compartmentalized approach and toward a more integrated one, where staff work in more innovative and agile ways to facilitate learning. School curricula should be governed by powerful inquiries that serve as the conceptual spine of the discipline, concentrating focus and organizing new information around a handful of big ideas. Student achievement should be motivated and measured by authentic tasks that require substantive problem solving, critical thinking, creativity, and collaboration. Classroom-level instruction should be designed to teach critical knowledge and skills to enable students to engage with the problem to be solved, the text to be read, or the expression to be created.

As we get ready to move from the fundamental flaws in the design of school to the renovation of the 21st century schoolhouse, the reader must become acclimated to the disequilibrium created when current habits have worn thin but no new ones have yet emerged. It is important to stay with complex problems without rushing for solutions, to dedicate time to acquiring knowledge about a given subject, to develop and pursue new ideas, and to demonstrate resilience when faced with setbacks. Setting yourself (and your colleagues) up to have more insights is an important part of the process. Robin Charbit and Charlie Kiefer (n.d.) have this to say:

> In a sense, the spaces between thoughts are the source of insight. If there are no spaces, there is little possibility of insight. Much of the thinking of people with a primarily Western background and lifestyle has the quality of being forced or pressed. Each thought is crushed into the next. When we want to solve a problem, we step on the gas and try to power through.

When we're engaged with this quality of thinking, though it might seem normal, the possibility of insight is reduced or eliminated. (paragraph 16)

As you continue on this journey, make sure that you aren't accelerating through the text by keeping the following ideas in mind:

- Give yourself time to sit with the three problems described in the opening chapters.
- Consider whether there are other problems that also reduce the effectiveness of our schools.
- Imagine what it would look like and feel like if students were no longer bored by school but energized by it.

The remainder of the book explores the possibilities, the components necessary to transform schools into 21st century learning organizations. If you are certain that schools are fundamentally fine and that it's the politicians, the parents, the college professors, the students, and the economists who have it wrong, the next 120 pages will probably be of little interest. Perhaps you will want to take more time to explore the problems through discussions at the local and national levels. The list of references at the end of this book may be useful to get you started on more research. If, however, you are skeptical but hopeful that your school (and schools in general) can become profoundly different, continue on. It's time that learning became joyful again for all of us.

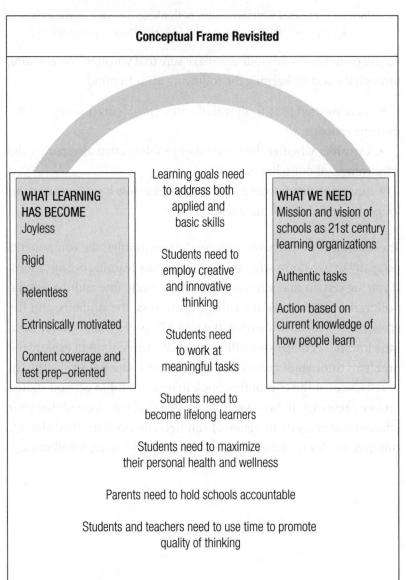

Conceptual Frame Revisited

Learning goals need to address both applied and basic skills

Students need to employ creative and innovative thinking

Students need to work at meaningful tasks

Students need to become lifelong learners

Students need to maximize their personal health and wellness

Parents need to hold schools accountable

Students and teachers need to use time to promote quality of thinking

WHAT LEARNING HAS BECOME
Joyless

Rigid

Relentless

Extrinsically motivated

Content coverage and test prep–oriented

WHAT WE NEED
Mission and vision of schools as 21st century learning organizations

Authentic tasks

Action based on current knowledge of how people learn

3

Transforming the 21st Century Schoolhouse into a Learning Organization

It is our American habit if we find the foundations of our educational structure unsatisfactory to add another story or wing. We find it easier to add a new study or course or kind of school than to recognize existing conditions so as to meet the need.

John Dewey

Reflection Question

What are we educating for? How can schools become true learning organizations?

The transformation of the 21st century schoolhouse must accommodate both the need to reengage the learner and the need to modernize our curriculum, assessment, and instructional practices to create a new model for our schools. But first we must establish what a learning organization is supposed to be:

• A learning organization clarifies the key goals that every learner is expected to achieve and the tasks that will measure achievement of the goals.

• A learning organization provides regular opportunities for learners to reexamine existing knowledge, assumptions, products, and processes to determine more innovative approaches, new areas of opportunity, and potential solution paths.

• A learning organization uses scientific knowledge of the brain and the way people learn to analyze the effectiveness of existing structures, practices, and designs and make needed improvements.

• A learning organization elicits the natural intelligence of the learner by exploring self-generated questions, areas of interest, and great ideas, and by devoting the time to pursue goals and develop skills.

In this chapter we will focus on the roles of mission and vision, two key components that communicate the goals of the learning organization with regard to the community it serves. First, we must *clarify the mission:* What are the learning goals that all students will accomplish as a result of their education in our school/school system? Second, we must *create a shared vision:* What will the realization of our mission look like?

The drafted language of our learning organization's mission and vision establishes a new model of reality based on what we believe to be true, necessary, and worthy in the teaching of our children. While there are many possible statements that will deliver on the promise of a 21st century school for the people in your community, I offer the following statement as a model:

> The mission of a 21st century learning organization is to engage all learn-
> ers in the acquisition of key knowledge and skills and the development of
> connections so that they can pursue powerful questions, tackle complex
> problems, collaborate with diverse people, imagine new possibilities, and
> communicate their ideas.

To support your own reading experience (and potential development/ refinement of these components), Chapters 3, 4, and 5 include if/then statements composed of proposed actions related to achieving the mission of a 21st century learning organization. An example follows:

IF we

- proclaim the learning goals of the school at every opportunity so that they become transparent to and trusted by every member of the school community as "the work" to be done;
- design structures, allocate resources, and implement practices that help realize the mission-driven goals;
- design tasks that both measure mission-driven goals and motivate students to achieve those goals; and
- design learning that is respectful and relevant to the learner, considering their prior knowledge, personal experiences, and current needs . . .

THEN we can engage all learners in the acquisition of key knowledge and skills and the development of connections so that they can pursue powerful questions, tackle complex problems, collaborate with diverse people, imagine new possibilities, and communicate their ideas.

These if/then statements provide a theory of action to help us identify those high leverage points that will focus the work at all levels of the learning organization. I have also included illustrative examples and processes from my consulting work in various districts to provide further clarification. Expect the research findings, quotations, and anecdotes to continue to come from a range of disciplines. The design of learning is not the sole property of the education community; we have much to learn from the evidence and insights provided by neuroscientists, cognitive psychologists, business leaders, artists, coaches, and authors.

Clarifying the Mission

Reflection Question

What are the learning goals that all students will accomplish as a result of their education in our school/school system?

IF we proclaim the learning goals of the school at every opportunity so they become transparent to and trusted by every member of the school community as "the work" to be done through

- articulating the handful of learning goals that will define the work of the school;
- posting the mission on the physical and virtual walls of the school;
- articulating connections between how today's agenda, lesson, or task relates to the larger mission (at the beginning of units of study, presentations, meetings, and school-based publications); and
- providing public and private forums for staff, students, and parents to articulate concerns or ideas that, if considered, would help the school achieve its mission . . .

THEN we can engage all learners in the acquisition of key knowledge and skills and the development of connections so that they can pursue powerful questions, tackle complex problems, collaborate with diverse people, imagine new possibilities, and communicate their ideas.

A mission statement brings clarity to the work of an organization. It provides a controlling focus for the projects we undertake, the choices we make, and the ideas we develop. While virtually all schools or school districts have mission statements, they often remain ceremonial fixtures on letterhead and posters rather than providing needed focus for individual and collective endeavors. When I ask teachers or administrators what their mission statement is, they frequently have to call a secretary, check their own Web site, or look through print material to find it. Once they have located it, they often discover that it does not have the clarity, passion, or focus needed to effect meaningful change. Trot out your existing mission statement—if you have one—and compare it to the list of key qualities found in Figure 3.1 to determine whether you are set to proceed, have a "diamond in the rough," or need to return to the drawing board and start over again.

If your mission statement already provides the powerful focus for the work of your 21st century learning organization, that's fantastic. Feel free to skip down to the next section. If you need assistance, continue to read on.

Figure 3.1	Qualities of an Effective Mission Statement

- Describes specific long-term goals for learners.
- Goes beyond specified knowledge and skills in established content standards to address larger aims of schooling (e.g., responsible citizenship, lifelong learning, critical thinking).
- Provides enough specificity to be addressed through the design of curriculum, assessment, and instruction.
- Key stakeholders are willing to commit to the scope of the mission statement.

Source: Zmuda, A., McTighe, J., Wiggins, G., & Brown, J. (2007). *Schooling by design: An ASCD action tool.* Alexandria, VA: ASCD.

Mission statements can be drafted in one day. All it takes is the right people in the room, relentless focus on what the students will accomplish (not on the adult work or areas outside of our direct control), and willingness to reconsider the true priorities in your community. Figure 3.2 shows an example mission statement that was created in just one day by the full administrator leadership team of a school district. The example in Figure 3.3 was created by a dozen teachers at a charter school in Georgia as an unexpected 20-minute tangent in a larger one-day meeting about student achievement.

The first step in the development of both examples was for participants to brainstorm all of the possible aims of a learning organization. They were given two parameters: they had to frame their ideas in terms of desired student learning, and they had to offer ideas they were willing to champion in their own work and within the larger school community. I have found that once people begin to think aloud together, hope flourishes in the abundance of opportunities and ideas that have perhaps always been present, but people have been too busy to contemplate.

Figure 3.2	Sample Mission Statement 1

Granby Public Schools Mission Statement: All students become powerful thinkers, effective collaborators, and compassionate contributors in preparation for success in a dynamic, interdependent world.

Powerful Thinker *How do I construct knowledge?*	Effective Collaborator *How do I engage others in a shared purpose?*	Compassionate Contributor *How do I demonstrate care for others and the world around us?*
• Define and pursue personal curiosity and complex problems • Develop a plan, evaluate and adjust based on feedback in order to accomplish a task or take on a challenge • Create innovative products or connections that contribute to quality of life or collective knowledge • Analyze text to construct meaning and make connections • Effectively communicate information and ideas for a given audience, purpose, or task • Reflect on and apply knowledge and wisdom to future inquiries	• Establish interdependence and collective accountability through collaboration on authentic and compelling tasks • Explore varied and divergent approaches to determine the most appropriate unified course of action • Provide and receive feedback from others to improve the process and the product • Produce coherent, quality work that maximizes individual contributions	• Demonstrate empathy, care, and connection for others • Identify needs of others and how to respond appropriately • Improve quality of life within the local or global community through service • Reflect on the impact of contributions on the community and self-concept • Champion causes and take actions that are vital to civic well-being • Conduct oneself in an ethical and respectful manner in interactions with others
As measured by . . . Academic, civic, and personal tasks of significance.		

Source: Granby Public Schools. Reprinted by permission.

Figure 3.3	Sample Mission Statement 2

All students engage in rigorous, standards-based tasks to be successful for the academic challenges at the most competitive high school programs. In the pursuit of academic excellence, students become motivated to pursue inquiries, to develop their individual talents, to engage others in conversation and collaborative projects, and to contribute to the wellness of their community.

Once there is a robust list, the challenge is how to identify priorities and unifying themes without marginalizing individual viewpoints or niche issues. There are three important considerations during the editing process. First, make sure that the mission statement does not reflect one personality, pedagogy, or segment of the school population—the goals must engage the work of every member of the school community. Do expect, however, that people will begin to raise quiet questions about whether these worthy aims are possible for every child. These concerns are important to participants because they are long-standing concerns that have been unearthed by the mission statement task. Second, make sure that the mission statement does not overreach. While we may have become accustomed to operating in hyperdrive to do as much as possible, learning organizations must clarify the key priorities that can truly be accomplished for all learners. Third, make sure that the power of the language does not become diluted. I have found that as the mission statement draws closer to completion, participants get nervous about how others might respond or how daunting it will be to do the work. It takes courage to finish the task, but also candor to realize that the moment the task is done (including seeking feedback from the larger community and making appropriate revisions), the real work begins.

Creating a Shared Vision

Reflection Question

What will the realization of our mission look like?

IF we design structures, allocate resources, and implement practices that help realize the mission-driven goals through

- establishing a guaranteed and viable curriculum that clarifies the goals of the particular course and how those goals tie into larger aims of the program and school curriculum;
- identifying and adopting 21st century skills as part of the foundation for how we think and work;

- nurturing interdisciplinary connections through opportunities to collaborate on research, service, problem solving, and idea creation; and
- striking a better balance between emphasis on rules and development of ideas . . .

THEN we can engage all learners in the acquisition of key knowledge and skills and the development of connections so that they can pursue powerful questions, tackle complex problems, collaborate with diverse people, imagine new possibilities, and communicate their ideas.

The key to envisioning the organization's mission requires the suspension of disbelief and constraints of accepted realities. Leaders must create space for fresh thought to emerge by providing an opportunity to imagine possibilities and develop good ideas with members of the school community. The work begins by encouraging participants to grow new ideas, free from the constraints of current practice. Far from being a "pie-in-the sky" exercise, these imaginings are a vital part of becoming a learning organization. Thomas Sergiovanni (2004) offers the following observation:

> Educators can be both hopeful and realistic as long as the possibilities for change remain open. Being realistic differs from facing reality in important ways. Facing reality means accepting the inevitability of a situation or circumstance; being realistic means calculating the odds with an eye toward optimism. (p. 34)

In order to develop a powerful conception of a learning organization, leaders should put together "heavyweight teams" composed of participants from different teams and with different job descriptions to rethink the possibilities without being restricted by individual interests. These teams will be created to accomplish a given task and then will be promptly disbanded so that more permanent "middleweight" teams (i.e., departments, grade-level teams, long-standing leadership committees) can implement the plan. Otherwise, "when the task of redesigning is given to teams of teachers who work within their departments, the projects are characterized by endless debates, begrudging compromises, and little change" (Christensen, Horn, & Johnson, 2008, p. 209).

Figure 3.4 contains a vision statement produced by a heavyweight team of education leaders in a public school in New York. Led by the superintendent and deputy superintendent, the team made the case for a 21st century schoolhouse that broke free from what they deemed a factory-style model of education. (Note: The quotations included in the first column come from Tony Wagner's book *The Global Achievement Gap* [2008].) The statement took this heavyweight team approximately five days of meeting time to develop. The easiest column to produce was the middle one; participants were quite clear as to how the current design of curriculum and instruction failed to ignite the passion, talent, and commitment of the student body. Achieving consensus on the key capacities also proved to be relatively easy. What was much more difficult to give voice to was what those capacities meant. Everyone values effective communication, including the classroom teachers who might suggest they already required that of their students. So what's the difference between the long-standing definition of effective communication and a more modern one? Again, you can see how they delineated between the two in Figure 3.4. The work produced by the heavyweight team cleared a path for staff to begin to evaluate the major gaps between existing practice and the vision of a 21st century schoolhouse, and opened the door for parents, community members, and school board members to help shape the future direction of curricular programs, effective use of newly acquired resources, and design of cornerstone tasks that will demonstrate student achievement in those capacities.

When people work together to conceive of new ways of combining existing knowledge, structures, and personnel, boundless potential, passion, and results are possible. In imagining and developing innovative products and solutions, business literature often advises two basic strategies: watch the consumer, and imagine what would be possible if there were no financial constraints. Set the first strategy in a school-based context: watch the students to see what they are naturally doing with a product or experience in order to customize it to fit their needs.

- Are they reading books of their own choice underneath their desks?
- Are they doing homework for one class while attending another?
- Are they copying down information from the board (blackboard, whiteboard, or SMART Board) so they have it in their notebooks?

- Are they waiting in the guidance counselor's office to find out about course selection availability for next year?
- Are they writing a letter to the principal to ask for permission to change a rule or pursue an idea?
- Are they networking with other students (on electronic devices or in physical spaces) to try to make sense of a problem they've been given?

Figure 3.4	Vision of the 21st Century Schoolhouse	
Key Capacities	**Factory-Model Compliance**	**21st Century Engagement**
Critical Thinking and Problem Solving "Work is no longer defined by your specialty; it's defined by the task or problem you and your team are trying to solve or the end goal you want to accomplish. Teams have to figure out the best way to get there—the solution is not prescribed. And so the biggest challenge for our front-line employees is having the critical-thinking and problem-solving skills they need to be effective in their teams—because nobody is there telling them exactly what to do. They have to figure it out."	• Follows procedures/ established processes to complete a task • Defers to "experts" to approach the task or get unstuck (teacher, other students, etc.) • Gives in to other people	• Shows persistence in the face of obstacles and difficulties • Shows resourcefulness, inventiveness • Seeks challenges and new ways of working • Sets clear goals and develops plans to achieve them • Makes own choices and defends/explains them • Accesses and analyzes information

Key Capacities	Factory-Model Compliance	21st Century Engagement
Personal Meaning "What exactly do I mean by a 'life purpose'? A purpose is an ultimate concern. It is the final answer to the question Why? Why are you doing this? Why does it matter to you? Why is it important? A purpose is a deeper reason for the immediate goals and motives that drive most daily behavior."	• Keeps out of trouble • Does what he or she is told to do when told to do it • Expresses frustration, anxiety, stress, about the current workload • Shows little enthusiasm for curricular activities • Lacks purpose, motivation • Conducts work at the surface level of the vocation, but not authentic or inspirational • Engages in a range of activities but no long-term commitment or depth	• Engages in work that is compelling • Designs/initiates learning that helps him or her pursue and develop passions both within curriculum and during extracurricular activities • Experiences deep satisfaction, sense of well-being as invested in deep work • Contributes to something or someone else larger than the self • Creates something of one's own • Engages in work for a longer period of time, strong level of commitment • Develops goals over time with support from adults in the learning community • Creates a network of peers to support the work • Attains personal fulfillment • Shows seriousness combined with lightheartedness

continued

Figure 3.4	Vision of the 21st Century Schoolhouse *(continued)*	
Key Capacities	**Factory-Model Compliance**	**21st Century Engagement**
Imaginative, Agile, Innovative Thinking "People's jobs change very rapidly. I've been at Dell a long time in similar sales and marketing functions—but what I do today versus what I did five or six years ago is completely different. To survive, you have to be flexible and adaptable and a lifelong learner. . . . And so some of the key competencies we hold employees accountable for include the ability to deal with ambiguity, the ability to learn on the fly, and strategic agility."	• A lot of jobs in schools haven't changed • Doesn't handle failure well • Extrinsic motivation drives individual efforts • Uses limited tools, resources, protocols to complete task	• Shows curiosity and imagination • Shows self-direction/initiative • Shows agility and adaptability • Uses varying products and processes to complete a task • Thinks about what to do when he/she gets stuck and how to get him- or herself out of it • Shows enthusiasm for ongoing learning • Is intrinsically motivated • Shows patience in the face of failure • Aims high and tries to give definition/pursue the unknown or uncertain • Is willing to take a riskier/less predictable course of action because the idea is worth pursuing • Has access to community of people, ideas, and tools

Key Capacities	Factory-Model Compliance	21st Century Engagement
Collaboration "Students have a naiveté about how work gets done in a corporate environment. They have a predisposition toward believing that everything is clearly outlined, and then people give directions, and then other people execute until there's a new set of directions. They don't understand the complexities of an organization—that boundaries are fluid, that rarely does one group have everything needed to get a job done. How do you solve a problem when people who own what you need are outside your organization or don't report to you, or the total solution requires a consortium of different people? How do you influence things that are out of your direct control?"	• Brainstorming is short so that students can do task assignment and get to work • Highly individualized very quickly • One child can carry the load for the group • Little tolerance for different ideas • Used to teach kids to "get along" with one another but not to become collectively interdependent	• Brainstorming to consider a broad range of ideas, options, and strategies before determining a course of action • Going outside of the organization to find out what's going on in a broader context/pursuit of a wider audience of ideas • End result may change—can be different from what was started with • Is able to identify/prioritize good ideas • Trusts learning • Responds/develops other students' ideas • Develops collective accountability • Requires a task that is a real challenge • Goes beyond interpersonal dynamics • Shows empathy, compassion • Shows social responsibility • Develops informed, caring, productive citizens

continued

Figure 3.4	Vision of the 21st Century Schoolhouse *(continued)*	
Key Capacities	Factory-Model Compliance	21st Century Engagement
Effective Communication "We are routinely surprised at the difficulty some young people have in communicating: Verbal skills, written skills, presentation skills. They have difficulty being clear and concise; it's hard for them to create focus, energy, and passion around the points they want to make. They are unable to communicate their thoughts effectively. You're talking to an exec, and the first thing you'll get asked if you haven't made it perfectly clear in the first sixty seconds of your presentation is, 'What do you want me to take away from this meeting?' They don't know how to answer that question."	• Expects but doesn't model effective communication • Rushes to cover teaching content . . . not enough time spent going deeply • Questions aren't rich and answers are often predetermined • Time constraints to producing communication do not encourage reflective, thoughtful thinking	• Student expression is well-rounded (verbal and nonverbal) • Shows good listening • Shows empathy • Essential questions clarify and focus purpose • Power of story is used to connect people • Crafts personal narrative • Uses story as an instrument of thought • Production of authentic tasks anchored to interests, passions, talents • Cultivates artistic/ design sensibility • Makes and defends proposals

Source: Nanunet Public Schools. Adapted by permission.

Now consider the second strategy: imagine what would be possible if money wasn't an issue? Picture a movie trailer for the school that we would love to teach in, to lead, to send our own children to. Tom Kelley (2001), general manager of IDEO, a design and development firm, contends that the imagining of a movie trailer helps participants clarify their thinking in a visual way and focus on what the product is and how it will capture the interest of the consumer. Think about what a group of educators, community members, and students would see if they sat down and imagined a new concept of school:

- What would the main office look like?
- What kind of furniture would be in the classrooms?
- What instructional tools would be at students' disposal?
- What instructional strategies would be used?
- What would the schedule look like?
- What sounds would we hear?
- What would conversations among students look like?
- What would parent-teacher conferences look like?
- What would the report card communicate?
- What would be the hallmarks of students' education?
- What would the diploma indicate?

For those of you who feel too "stuck" in problems to imagine possibilities, an effective alternative is to use those concerns as the basis for the vision. A charter school staff sat down with me and in 30 minutes made a long list of all the things that were "wrong" and made it difficult for them to teach and for students to learn. We then revised the list so that it was limited to those concerns within their locus of control. The list makes up the first column of the table in Figure 3.5. The next step was to produce the third column, not the second one. The staff were *not* asked to offer any potential solutions; instead, they were invited to imagine what school would look like if the serious concern no longer existed. It was fascinating to observe how the conversation went from total clarity about the serious concerns to quiet confusion in the imagining phase. We spend much of our time stewing in our problems with no picture in our heads of what a healthier, happier, more energized learning environment would look like. The third and final step was to produce the middle column; to accomplish this, the staff brainstormed ideas about what actions they could take to make the third column possible.

When the staff left that day, their serious concerns were as real as they were when they came in the room, but their thinking about those concerns had shifted. What had previously seemed an immutable reality had opened up for improvement.

Below are three steps to take to clarify your own thinking with your colleagues about your vision for your school. I strongly recommend that you identify some kind of protocol for this process so that ideas can emerge for collective consideration.

Step 1: Create the Space for Conversation

This type of thinking is best done with a group of 3 to 12 people who are comfortable enough with one another to think aloud (create, develop, and analyze an idea together) but not so comfortable with one another that they think alike. The focus of these conversations should be clearly established in advance, using questions such as the following:

- What is the goal? This can be in the form of a problem statement, question, or improvement item.
- What is the role of the members of the group?
- What are the parameters for the conversation (rules, time limits)?
- Who will be the audience for the ideas that emerge?

Ideally the conversation will be scheduled at a time of day when people have the energy and the agility to think—this kind of task is not easy to pull off at 7:00 in the morning or 4:00 in the afternoon.

Step 2: Insist on a True Brainstorm

Brainstorming requires skill development and organizational consistency, along with a high quantity of ideas—the crazier the better. The team should feel comfortable to suggest whatever comes to mind, without inhibition. A brainstorming session should last for around an hour, and should provoke in team members "optimism and a sense of opportunity that can carry [the team] through the darkest and most

Figure 3.5	A Vision of the Ideal School	
Because of our serious concerns about . . .	We propose that we develop . . .	Which would result in . . .
Student disengagement as learners means that they are passive or "tuned out" during instruction and inconsistent in their completion of assignments	• More student-directed, independent, collaborative tasks • More "student talk" in classrooms where they are expected to speak respectfully and professionally to one another (appropriate use of academic vocabulary, ability to listen and respond, ability to think aloud together to complete a task) • Engagement with higher-order questions with one another (instead of being led to an answer by a teacher) • Student-led conferences • More focus on the nutritional health (food, water, sleep) and physical exercise of students to improve their ability to focus in the classroom • More deliberate mechanisms to place students in classrooms so that they are in an optimal learning environment	• Greater energy levels in classrooms since staff don't have to drag students along, but rather allow them to learn from each other • Greater opportunities to strengthen relationships through identifying and pursuing personal interests of students as a way of achieving learning goals • Greater success on independent tasks

continued

Figure 3.5	A Vision of the Ideal School *(continued)*	
Because of our serious concerns about . . .	**We propose that we develop . . .**	**Which would result in . . .**
Students who are carrying adult responsibilities and stressors outside of school, which affect their ability to focus during school	• Greater staff consistency about how to teach the whole child without lowering expectations for learning • Staff vigilance about how we speak about our students to model our faith in and commitment to their potential • More opportunities for students (and parents) to receive enrichment opportunities through the school	• Increased student accountability for their behavior and actions • Less of staff "talking down" and over-scaffolding of learning and more expectation to rise up, be resilient • Increased partnerships with parents/grandparents to support learning at home and to grow the interests and future goals of students
Students being unprepared for the next grade level because of lack of program coherence or development of necessary knowledge and skills	• "Wraparound" tasks to sharpen curricular focus in each grade level • Maps of standards for the grade level/course • Diagnostic and formative assessments to more accurately gauge achievement and tailor instruction • Increased consistency in how grades are determined so that an *A* indicates excellence based on the standards (as separate from progress made or work ethic)	• Less of a need for reteaching because of greater retention of knowledge and skills and greater ability to tackle new/unfamiliar challenges, problems, and texts

Because of our serious concerns about . . .	We propose that we develop . . .	Which would result in . . .
Students who are not consistently held to high expectations, which results in a lessening of personal responsibility and an inappropriate level of comfort	• Authentic assessments that require risk taking, problem solving with no obvious solution path, and opportunities for students to revise their work to meet performance expectations • Schoolwide rubrics that are consistently used (and collaboratively scored) to evaluate student work • Explicit teaching of social skills (etiquette, questioning, appropriate expression of frustration) • Greater focus on the quality of thinking in addition to coming up with the right answer/viable solution/legitimate interpretation	• A culture of rigor and high expectations where it is normal to have to think and work hard and success is defined by achievement • Students who are able to experience discomfort, ambiguity, and uncertainty as they are working on significant tasks • Students who are able to get the "wrong answer" without feeling defeated or embarrassed • Students who seek out more difficult challenges because they are pushing themselves to improve
Students are not expected to be brilliant; mediocrity is considered successful	• Expectation that the sharing of accomplishments is a learning opportunity for the audience (not something to be tolerated or dismissed) • Expectation that the sharing of accomplishments is an obligation of the achiever to elevate the quality of work in the school	• A greater percentage of students in the "exceeds expectation" category of standardized tests • Examples of brilliance displayed on the walls of the school • Public recognition of great work based on achievement (not on behavior management)

continued

Figure 3.5	A Vision of the Ideal School (*continued*)	
Because of our serious concerns about . . .	We propose that we develop . . .	Which would result in . . .
Students do not see the potential of their lives and exhibit uncertainty about the trajectory of their lives and the impact that is possible on the world	• Students who are being prepared for something bigger than "the tests" as the focus of their daily work • More effective ways of diagnosing and meeting the needs of students to improve psychological and emotional health • Support groups for students and parents around shared psychological and emotional health issues	• More pride in their current work and excitement about future potential
Students do not have strong literacy skills, which impacts achievement in all subject areas	• Greater coherence in reading, writing program • Uniform expectation for nonfiction process writing • Uniform expectation for becoming independent, voracious readers • High-frequency, high-stakes academic vocabulary lists and common instructional and assessment approach for development of fluency	• More sophisticated explanations of their thinking using appropriate academic vocabulary • Increased ability to comprehend problems and nonfiction texts/technical writing

Because of our serious concerns about . . .	We propose that we develop . . .	Which would result in . . .
Students do not understand how to learn; there is no clarity about how the brain works, their own learning style, or how to handle learning when it doesn't come easily	• Learner profiles to uncover how each individual student works best and show how to leverage that capacity in the design of instruction and assessment • Uniform use of essential questions to spark and deepen learning within the subject area (questions are consistently used within and across grade levels) • Explicit teaching of how to become better at "this" (increased fluency, increased capacity to make connections, growth mind-set) • Staff modeling of own learning, development, and resilience • Expectation and opportunities for revision of work • Inclusion of biographies/autobiographies in every subject area to model what "greats" endure on the road to accomplishments	• Greater ability to troubleshoot and address own learning problems • More student-directed self-differentiation to complete a given task • Greater ability to communicate "How I did that/How I arrived at that" as a basis for synthesizing process, improving performance, and celebrating accomplishments • Greater frequency of connections that students independently make between what they are learning in the curriculum and their broader knowledge

pressure-tinged stages of a project" (Kelley, 2001, p. 56). Usually, the first flurry of ideas is quite predictable and draws on established knowledge. When wild suggestions begin to emerge, allow the space for them to be truly heard.

I witnessed the effectiveness of this type of brainstorming during a series of community forums held in a school district that was working on the development of a new mission statement. In the first forum, community members were asked simply to describe what they wanted from their schools—what were the "nonnegotiables" of a 21st century public school education? The responses were very straightforward and often stemmed from either individuals' own childhood experiences or from the type of children they were raising or had raised. Interestingly enough, most of what the community members wanted was part of the existing system. When prodded to "think outside of the box," very few new ideas were offered, and none of them captured the interest of the group. In the second forum, we took a very different approach. Community members were arranged in circles—groups of 8 to 12—and informed that the purpose of the conversation was to "think outside of the box," which meant that they were to generate ideas, the more the better. They were instructed that there were only two rules: first, to frame their comments with the starting phrase "What if . . ." and, second, to pause three seconds before the next person in the circle spoke. The intent of these two rules was to slow down the conversation so that the ideas could be conceived, shared, and developed without psychic stress. What resulted was remarkable, not only in content but also in quality of conversation. People visibly slowed down their thinking, became more relaxed as the rounds continued, and became more engaged in what they each had to say. Following are some of the "what ifs" the community came up with:

- What if high school had no bells at all and experiences were allowed to continue until they were done?
- What if we abolished grades altogether and just used multiple assessments across content areas that allowed students to demonstrate learning without it being translated into a score?
- What if we had a more project-based design, where students rotated through tasks instead of rotating through courses?
- What if students experienced fearless curiosity about their learning and weren't concerned about the grades/parameters?
- What if students were challenged every day?
- What if students and teachers crafted the curriculum together?
- What if students left high school knowing who they are?

- What if it were valued/encouraged to experiment, take risks, and have the ability to fail and not be penalized for it?
- What if every meeting/lesson had a point that everyone knew and believed was important?
- What if students recognized that school is part of their real world?

The power of the conversation was evident in the new avenues of thinking as well as the impact of the experience. Community members thanked us for the opportunity to participate and expressed the wish that these experiences would happen more often, and some even volunteered to engage in further development work. In addition, the district leaders gained a significant treasure trove of ideas as well as ability to glean common themes in community responses that led to the development of the new mission statement.

Step 3: Develop Great Ideas Without Getting Stuck on "One Right Answer"

Reflection Question

What do you do when a promising idea emerges? How do you collaborate with others to develop it further?

The power of the process of developing vision statements is that it brings to life the possibilities for our students and ourselves. Figure 3.6 presents a protocol for developing ideas that allows teams to thoughtfully consider them and work toward their implementation.

Dreaming aloud can become an organizational habit, especially when leaders provide the necessary resources to "green-light" promising practices. A powerful example of this happened on a one-day consulting project at a regional Board of Cooperative Educational Services (BOCES) in upstate New York. The folks in attendance (approximately half a dozen leaders) were worried about the future longevity of robust library programs given fiscal realities and limited administrative support.

The "problem" quickly became clear: because of limited resources the impact of the library-classroom was being significantly curtailed, which, in turn, made it difficult to reinstate funding because of the limited impact (and so the downward spiral). I asked the participants to stop trying to defend the program and instead to define it. What would the "ideal" library program look like? How would it function? The statement in Figure 3.7 was crafted during a one-hour brainstorm and a three-hour intensive writing session.

Figure 3.6	Protocol for Developing Ideas

1. Participants craft a preliminary idea that they find personally compelling *and* in service to the work of a 21st century school (this can be done in the opening 10 minutes of the meeting or in advance of the meeting).
2. A participant explains the idea without being interrupted.
3. The other participants then pose clarifying questions to better understand the nature and scope of the idea. The person who introduced the idea responds to the questions to clarify and develop the idea both for the proposer and for the group. *Note: During this time, there is to be no discussion of management/ implementation concerns or past failures.*
4. The idea is summarized by the recorder.
5. The process is continued around the room until all ideas have been discussed.
6. After the meeting, participants read the record produced of the ideas and rank the ideas on a scale of 1 to 5 based on how personally compelling they find the idea and the extent to which it will further the work of the school.
7. The top-ranked ideas become the focus for the next development meeting.

The result of this work is a clear picture of what a quality library program could look like and a revitalized approach about how to achieve it. Each descriptor becomes an opportunity to develop into more good ideas—the creation of extracurricular programs, online information spaces, mobile furniture groupings, etc.—in order to realize the vision. The participants still had the same problems to face, but much more clarity about the short-term actions and long-term planning needed to effect real change.

Figure 3.7	The Mission of the 21st Century Library

The 21st century library is a learning hub—a shared learning space where learners come together in their pursuit of knowledge and understanding of themselves and their world. Their work in an information-rich environment requires curiosity, passion, tolerance, and persistence in order to navigate, organize, and make sense of information so that learners can create knowledge that is of significance.

A "library" includes those physical and virtual spaces (including library classrooms, video-conferencing/production space, computer labs, outdoor courtyards, website, portals) that are designed by the school to promote information literacy and technology as well as appreciation of aesthetics.

Evidence that a learning hub exists includes (but is not limited to) the following characteristics:
1. The walls of the space
   a. Evidence of student learning on tasks designed by the classroom staff as well as independent journeys crafted by the students
   b. Clearly state the expectations and curricular goals (AASL, NSTE) for the shared space so that learning is possible for everyone within it and people operate in an ethical, responsible manner
   c. Color of and text on the walls are conducive to learning—calming, inviting, thoughtful effect on the learner
2. The organization of the furniture, equipment, and technology
   a. Comfortable chairs that invite learners to stay and read
   b. Different organizational setups to promote different types of learning: collaborative space for dialogue and problem solving; solitary space for intense study, reflection, reading; conference space for mini-lessons, meetings, and forum; class space for when a whole class is working together on a given task
   c. Tools that are designed for learners to use to facilitate their shared thinking and knowledge construction—laptop/LCD to project their thinking; flip charts/markers, Post-it notes, and scrap paper; access to copier machine; access to wikis, blogs, shared electronic resources; ability to transport their work to and from school (portable media devices, email accounts for students, remote access to work from home); access to computers (lab, mobile laptops)
3. The organization of exhibits
   a. Connections organized around themes and topics currently being explored in curricular and co-curricular areas
   b. Exhibits (virtual or in the library space) that are highly responsive to what is going on in the world today (both in the school and literally in the world)
   c. Exhibits designed around student interests, preferences, talents

continued

Figure 3.7	The Mission of the 21st Century Library (*continued*)

4. The access to tools, resources, materials
   a. Signage that clearly demarks sections of the space so that it sponsors independent navigation (this applies to the library website as well)
   b. Prominent display/access to established procedures for: navigating non-fiction text, computer searches, research process (Big 6), citing sources, asking questions, ethical and responsible use of information
   c. Consistent review of access policies to ensure that students are sufficiently trained in the use of current electronic resources that are prevalent in post-secondary life (education, workplace, and social interactions)
   d. Consistent formal and informal learning opportunities to independently navigate electronic resources and data manipulation tools (both new ones and more established ones)
5. The communication of learning
   a. Ability for students to communicate with one another directly either through the exchange of ideas and information in dialogue or through the posting of learning (creation of wikis, blogs, book reviews, podcasting)
   b. Opportunities to showcase student learning through formal and informal demonstrations/performances
   c. The policies
   d. Clear policy for acceptable use of technology that is enforced and tended to by all users of the space
   e. Restricted access to sites is based on a constant balance of the ability of learners to navigate space pursuing their curiosities/exploration with the responsibility to block them from places they should not be
   f. Circulation policy (both how many and also access to sources not currently available on site) encourages every learner to check out those materials they want to explore
   g. Implementation of cyber-safety curricula to protect students from bullying, scams, harassment, identity theft

Source: School Library System E2CC BOCES. Reprinted by permission.

One of the most depressing things about staff meetings is how quickly people can destroy a new idea. Oftentimes, a new proposal is swiftly crushed by a litany of reasons why it cannot and should not be done. This inability to develop an idea stems from the compulsion to figure out how to implement it in the existing system before allowing people the necessary time to cultivate it into a compelling vision. So many good ideas are tentatively shared and then dropped (or obliterated) out of fear that they are not possible, worthy, or popular. Many of the educators I meet lack not imagination but faith in their schools and in one another to give those ideas a real chance. But dreaming aloud can become an organizational habit, especially when leaders provide the necessary resources to "green-light" promising practices.

The largest obstacle to this process can be the shackles we place on our own thinking. If every new idea is instantly deemed "impossible" because we don't have the funds, policies in place, parental support, technology, training, or time, attempting to verbalize and elucidate our vision for our organization will produce frustration rather than clarity or optimism. But if, using whatever protocols are necessary, educators sit and imagine together for a while, not only will fresh thinking likely emerge but energy levels will rise. Imaging what you could accomplish!

Moving to Action

Reflection Question

How committed are we to actually doing something to realize our hopes?

There are real limits to any great idea: theoretical "right answers" can be dysfunctional in practice, innovative approaches can become outdated, and improved methods can be less satisfying than habitual routines. The key to improved system performance, then, is to continue to imagine ways for all learners to achieve stated learning goals in an environment that is dynamic, personalized, and supportive. One of my fundamental beliefs is that change begins with the individual—you, my reader. We cannot wait for the day when the stars align, when budgets are flush, or when colleagues are willing. We must begin with being the change we wish to see in our classrooms and our schools. The "Moving to Action" section of this and subsequent chapters describes what can be done at various levels of the learning organization to create greater clarity about the purpose of schooling.

What Can One Teacher Do?

- Examine grade-level and course curricula to identify the main learning goals that focus student learning.
- Articulate those goals on the walls of the classroom and in communication with families.
- Identify models of quality work that show what achievement of goals looks like both at the developmental level of the students as well as in "greats" in the given subject area.
- Make explicit connections between the main learning goals and the daily lessons.
- Review all classroom policies, structures, and furniture arrangements to ensure they support identified goals.
- Collaborate with colleagues to strengthen coherence among goals in your classroom and those in the prior and following years to strengthen transitions and effectiveness.

What Can One Department or Program Do?

- Develop a mission statement that establishes the larger aims of the department/program in both its current form and its future conception. Following are examples of such statements from work done with all the department coordinators in a school district.

  – *Health.* The health education program encourages students to make informed choices, to accept responsibility for their personal health habits, and to realize the profound effect these lifestyle choices will have on the quality of their lives in the future.

  – *Art.* Through the application of the elements of art, students will examine and create visual pieces to solve problems, express feelings, and communicate ideas.

  – *English Language Arts.* Students will acquire the skills to appreciate and analyze the English language as a creative, informative, and persuasive tool to be effective communicators.

– *Technology Education.* Students will develop expertise in problem solving and communicate ideas through various media as they use advanced technological tools to take an idea from conception to completion.

– *Math.* Students will strategically apply mathematical concepts and skills by working with complex problems in order to develop their logical reasoning and ability to create expression that is both concrete and abstract.

• Use mission statements to drive the long-range development of the department or program in the creation of new courses, revision or elimination of existing courses, development of authentic tasks and related scoring tools, collaborative analysis of student work, and budgetary requests for additional staffing and resources.

• Identify opportunities for staff and students to "see" how what they are learning relates to what is required in postsecondary education programs and professional vocations via guest speakers, distance learning, field trips, mentorship network, conferences, and so forth.

What Can One School Do?

• Identify key actions in light of organizational, leadership, and instructional commitments to improve student achievement.

• Develop a time line to chunk initiatives based on urgency, resources needed, and increasing complexity of the work.

• Keep the work relentlessly focused on the key actions over a minimum of three years so that staff, parents, and students trust the seriousness of the endeavor.

The leadership team of one Philadelphia charter school outlined key actions that tied the important initiatives that staff had begun within the past three years to newer initiatives, showing the interrelatedness of the efforts and the expectations at every level of the learning organization (see Figure 3.8).

Figure 3.8	Sample Long-Term Key Actions to Improve Student Achievement from a Pennsylvania Charter School

Organizational Level
Structures, Practices, and Policies
• Develop a coherent, guaranteed, standards-driven curriculum for grades 6–12
• Develop scope and sequence and pacing guides to ensure that what is designed is taught and assessed
• Develop meaningful and authentic summative assessments that measure curricular goals
• Develop scoring tools that establish criteria for quality work
• Develop and query our databases about student achievement to identify and remedy gaps in achievement and inform resource allocation with all deliberate speed
• Provide students and parents with clear information about *achievement* on curricular goals separate from effort and growth
• Develop tasks and processes that provide students with opportunities to plan for the future through the pursuit of their individual passions, areas of interest, and post-secondary aspirations

Leadership Level
Administrators, Village Leads, and Curriculum Coordinators
• Clarify how roles and responsibilities relate to student achievement
• Lead the effort to create a culture that sustains the collective energy through a combination of strategies
• Implement semi-annual performance review for all leadership positions based on established criteria
• Engage staff in necessary conversations modeling appropriate professionalism, open-mindedness, and persistence
• Provide candid feedback about steps to be taken to improve student achievement and hold staff accountable for implementation
• Focus supervision of learning to improve student achievement and develop staff accountability for results (as measured by state tests and locally developed tasks)

Instructional Level
Teachers, Aides, and Guidance Counselors
• Establish and communicate big goals for student achievement
• Implement strategies and structures consistently that emphasize cooperative learning
• Use scoring tools to provide students with regular and specific feedback about the progress of the achievement toward big goals
• Provide students with regular/consistent opportunities to revise or redo work informed by teacher feedback and recommendations
• Find ways to overcome obstacles in student achievement regardless of the complexity or difficulty of the issue
• Lead the effort to create a culture that sustains the collective energy through a combination of strategies

- Tailor instruction appropriately to respect the prior knowledge, native language, cultural frame of reference, and personal preferences of every learner.
- Use established and fluid partnerships to collaborate on the design, delivery, and assessment of student learning
- Effectively use existing resources and support systems for struggling students in a proactive manner

Source: Marianna Charter School, Philadelphia, Pennsylvania. Reprinted by permission.

What Can One System Do?

- Reexamine job descriptions to make explicit connections between the mission-driven goals and individual roles and responsibilities.

- Reexamine committee, team, and task force composition and focus to reaffirm connections between the mission-driven goals and collective agenda.

- Focus staff meeting time on the analysis of student work to determine the gaps between current performance and mission-driven goals and work to identify appropriate instructional and organizational remedies.

- Use mission and vision language to engage school community in the articulation of concerns that must be addressed in order to achieve larger systems goals. An example of this process was carried out in one Connecticut school system (see Figure 3.9): A task force composed of staff, students, and parents worked for one year to develop a vision of the graduate that captures the aims of a 21st century learning organization committed to high achievement and student well-being.

Figure 3.9	Vision of the Graduate

[We] are committed to preparing students to function effectively in an interdependent global community. Therefore, in addition to acquiring a core body of knowledge*, all students will develop their individual capacities to:
- Pose and pursue substantive questions
- Critically interpret, evaluate, and synthesize information

*The core body of knowledge is established in local curricular documents which reflect national and state standards as well as workplace expectations.

continued

Figure 3.9	**Vision of the Graduate** (*continued*)

- Explore, define, and solve complex problems
- Communicate effectively for a given purpose
- Advocate for ideas, causes, and actions
- Generate innovative, creative ideas and products
- Collaborate with others to produce a unified work and/or heightened understanding
- Contribute to community through dialogue, service, and/or leadership
- Conduct themselves in an ethical and responsible manner
- Recognize and respect other cultural contexts and points of view
- Pursue their unique interests, passions, and curiosities
- Respond to failures and successes with reflection and resilience
- Be responsible for their own mental and physical health

Once the vision was drafted, representatives of the task force held a series of forums with their constituents (students led student meetings, parents led parent meetings, etc.) to articulate concerns and determine the extent to which those concerns posed significant impediments to realizing the vision. By leading the larger school community through this gap-analysis exercise, participants not only became more invested in the language of the vision, but they also realized that the priorities of the school district from this point forward would be driven by these shared learning goals.

The Concerns Exercise
I'm most concerned about _____ (practice, policy, structures, curriculum, programs) because _____ (tied to the Vision of the Graduate).
1. Context
2. Task Directions
   - Name the concern
   - Connect to component(s) of the vision statement
   - Explain the reasoning behind the connection
   - (Optional) Offer potential solutions
3. Examples (selected specifically for the stakeholder group)
4. Rules (if any)

Sample responses:
- I'm most concerned about the policy used about the weighting of grades at the high school because it mitigates against students *pursuing their unique interests, passions, and curiosities*. Because the weighting system rewards students more for getting an "A" in an AP and Honors class, students who take classes with no AP or Honors designation are actually penalized for electing to take courses which they find personally fascinating but have a negative impact on class rank and honor roll.
- I'm most concerned about the lack of a meaningful vocational education program which inhibits their opportunity to *explore, define, and solve complex problems* as well as *pursue their unique interests, passions, and curiosities*. There are a growing number of students who need to prepare for the workplace because high school is designed for students who intend to go on to traditional four-year college programs.

> - I'm most concerned about the current practice of assigning graduation credit based on seat time because the goal of schooling is *to acquire core knowledge and develop individual capacities*. Students should be awarded credits based on demonstrated competencies. The time it takes for students to meet the prerequisites within the standard 6 block day inhibits their ability to *pose and pursue substantive questions and pursue their unique interests, passions, and curiosities.*

Source: Milford Public Schools. Reprinted by permission.

Conclusion

The renovation of the 21st century schoolhouse requires the boldness to permanently disrupt the status quo. Educators must create structures to develop ideas so that fresh thinking occurs with greater frequency and receives a better reception when shared. Pairing this habitual practice with the gritty determination to get results amplifies powerful ideas to close the gap between the vision and the status quo. Every institution has the potential to achieve an "idealized" vision but must consider a range of possible innovations that are most likely to cause results.

This renovation also requires what Abrahamson refers to as the "creative recombination" elements. "Change with less pain involves knowing what already exists in the system that can be revised, as well as knowing how you can redeploy and recombine existing elements in the system into new configurations" (quoted in Fullan, Hill, & Crévola, 2006, p. 14). Michael Fullan (Fullan et al., 2006) suggests that leaders look both within their own organization to previous initiatives attempted as well as outward to new practices:

> Education reform is at a stage where many of the components of successful large-scale reform are evident in schools' collective basements. One half of the solution is to seek out and identify the critical elements that need to be in place; the other half is combining them creatively. This is not simply a job of alignment, but rather one of establishing dynamic connectivity among the core elements. (p. 15)

Educators know from experience that oftentimes the most innovative ideas become saddled with organizational restrictions (e.g., bell schedule, funding structures, teacher and administrator union concerns, assessment requirements) to the point where the original concept is no longer appealing. Distance learning equipment that was purchased by school districts decades ago with the promise of expanding course offerings with minimal budgetary cost largely gathered dust. Standards-based report cards were developed to improve the quality of information that parents received about student achievement, but the complexity of many reports caused parents to wish for a return to the days when their children received a letter or number grade along with a handwritten commentary about their child's performance. Leaders must expect this challenge and develop plans to shepherd a true "disruption" to the status quo. According to Christensen and colleagues (2008):

> In the language of disruption, here is what this means: unless top managers actively manage this process, their organization will shape every disruptive innovation into a sustaining innovation—one that fits the processes, values, and economic model of the existing business—because organizations cannot naturally disrupt themselves. This is a core reason why incumbent firms are at a disadvantage relative to entrant companies when disruptive innovations emerge. And it explains why computers haven't changed schools. (p. 75)

Changes mean little if they do not translate into progress toward or realization of mission-driven learning goals.

4

Designing Tasks to Focus Student Work and Measure Mission-Driven Goals

Reflection Question

What is learning most naturally like? How can we open up the opportunities for this in our schools?

Students first arrive at the schoolhouse door full of wonderment, questions, and a desire to explore the world. But when the work of school turns to the coverage and testing of new knowledge in isolation from prior knowledge and the real world, students lose sight of the purpose of school. Instead of looking for satisfaction from the simple joy of learning, they begin to rely on less satisfying, more superficial sources of meaning, such as good grades or making parents happy. Robert Fried (2005) makes a moving case for ceasing "the game of school"—a game where teachers and students "earnestly comply with what they feel to be their duty":

> When we allow ourselves to gear ourselves up so as to complete school tasks that have little meaning for us aside from the value of getting them done and over with, we lose touch with our own learning spirit. We become alienated from the natural learning desires and inquisitiveness

within us. We tend to become compliant rather than creative, docile
instead of courageous, inwardly passive instead of assertively engaged,
cynical at a time in life when we should be idealistic. (p. 14)

Students thrive when they have the opportunity to engage in curricular tasks as well as those that they personalize and pursue because
of their own areas of passion, direction, and purpose. Rigor and relevance not only come from the prior knowledge, life experience, and
cultural frame of reference of the learner, but also emanate from the
work that experts do in the field and that citizens do as part of their
civic responsibility.

IF we design tasks that both measure mission-driven goals and
motivate students to achieve those goals through

- making creativity a central component of student problem solving,
product development, and expression;
- providing opportunities for students to personalize the work
based on their interests, preferred ways of working, prior knowledge,
self-generated inquiries, and future aspirations;
- making revision a universal policy of the classroom, school, or
system so that all students have the right and the opportunity to improve
their work based on clear feedback and support from staff;
- developing grading and reporting systems that provide transparent
measures of achievement; and
- establishing electronic repositories that house completed tasks so
that students graduate from school with a record of their accomplishments . . .

THEN we can engage all learners in the acquisition of key knowledge
and skills and the development of connections so that they can pursue
powerful questions, tackle complex problems, collaborate with diverse
people, imagine new possibilities, and communicate their ideas.

The first half of this chapter explores five key task characteristics that
should inform the design of real-world tasks:

- Tasks should be authentic.
- Tasks should meet a shared definition of quality.

- Tasks should result in a record of accomplishment.
- Tasks should engender struggle.
- Tasks should be enjoyable.

When these characteristics are addressed through the design of tasks, scoring tools, and grading and reporting practices, assessment plays a much more meaningful role in the learning organization. It not only provides more powerful evidence for student achievement of mission-driven goals, it also strengthens clarity of purpose and the connections between schoolwork and "real" work.

Tasks Should Be Authentic

Authenticity refers to the degree to which the task mirrors the work processes and formats that govern the work of professionals in a field or discipline. This authenticity requires much more than a "hands-on" experience, integration of technology, or identification of an audience for the work. Learners must have the opportunity to develop their thinking and produce important work using appropriate tools and conventions. The three examples below illustrate the work that goes into creating authentic tasks and incorporating them into the curriculum; we will observe grades 6–12 school staff, high school academy staff, and K–12 science staff.

Authenticity in Grades 6–12

In this case study, middle and high school staff in several subject areas were working to improve the quality of summative assessments through the articulation of performance standards. While staff had extraordinarily high expectations of their students, school leaders believed that the existing assessment practices focused too much on recall, surface-level explanations of thinking, and decontextualized problem solving and communication tasks. We started by creating performance standards in each subject area to delineate what quality tasks—tasks that are authentic to the discipline, require transfer of learning, and incorporate

21st century skills—should measure. Listed below are the standards developed for math, science, English, and history.

Math

Students should be able to

- Analyze a problem situation to identify patterns and make predictions.
- Create and execute a solution path(s) to determine the most effective or reasonable solution.
- Analyze and justify the solution to effectively communicate results.
- Create questions or goals based on (but not limited to) connections to prior knowledge that stimulate further exploration or analysis.

Science

Students should be able to

- Use observations and integrated knowledge to generate investigable questions and/or goals that stimulate exploration.
- Generate and evaluate hypotheses that make testable predictions.
- Design investigations using appropriate scientific tools, resources, and representations to generate evidence that addresses the original questions and hypotheses.
- Analyze data and arrive at justifiable conclusions that are effectively communicated to an audience.
- Engage in ongoing exchange of information, ideas, and approaches to develop a plan, communicate findings, and/or evaluate the validity of results.

English

Students should be able to

- Create questions or connections that enrich and stimulate further exploration/analysis.
- Articulate the circumstances, evidence, and train of thought that led to the interpretation.
- Evaluate the validity of a range of interpretations to deepen or challenge their own assumptions/conclusions.
- Conceive a product that reflects individual voice and new insight.

- Conceive, create, and revise a text to make sure it is appropriate for the audience.

History

Students should be able to

- Analyze a given situation to identify patterns and make predictions.
- Assess the validity of information and the intent of the individual/organization presented in any text.
- Adapt the way they explain and support their ideas based on audience and task.
- Pose questions and examine underlying assumptions to construct meaning and broaden understanding.
- Collaborate with people of various backgrounds and perspectives to generate ideas and achieve a common goal.

The next step was for each department to identify or create performance tasks that would provide students the opportunity to do this work. Staff adopted a critical friends protocol, which guided their conversations in subject-area teams as they evaluated good performance tasks in order to determine alignment with performance standards and, based on that analysis, discussed how to improve the task. Included below is one example of how this process triggered a redesign of an existing task in honors biology.

Original Question

The existence of variation within a species is a key component of evolutionary change.

    a) Why is variation so important for evolution?

    b) What are the molecular and genetic causes of variation?

Explanation for Redesign

The original question addresses some very important and fundamental aspects of evolutionary theory and the integration between molecular biology and evolution. When we first asked the question on a final exam, we received many tangential and unexpected responses, showing that the question was too broad and unfocused.

We wanted to rework the question entirely, still addressing some of the important concepts, but providing more focus and more connection to the performance-based assessment design standards. We also wanted the students to have the opportunity to be creative in applying the concepts they were learning over the course of the semester.

The idea for the redesign came from a scenario I remembered from my evolution course in graduate school, in which an entire population of Laysan ducks was founded from a single female. The redesigned question (below) emphasizes the process of evolution and the role of variation, and gives the students many options for approaching the question while applying evolutionary concepts. It addresses the science department design standards involving generating hypotheses, analyzing data, arriving at justifiable conclusions, and communicating effectively to an audience.

The next step will be to design a grading rubric to take into account the variety of possible responses that will still show correct application of the concepts. We will also end up having to rework the rest of the exam or come up with creative solutions for administering the exam (e.g., in parts over several days), because the performance-based tasks we are asking students to perform will take more time.

Redesigned Question

The Laysan duck is the most endangered species of waterfowl in the United States. There are approximately 500 birds living in the Hawaiian Islands, in two distinct populations. One of the populations, at the Midway Atoll National Wildlife Refuge (NWR), was founded from only approximately 26 breeding individuals.

As a scientist working for the U.S. Fish and Wildlife Service, your job is to develop a plan to foster the recovery of the Laysan duck. You are focused on the Midway Atoll NWR population. Your superiors at the U.S. Fish and Wildlife Service have two questions for you to answer before you embark on a detailed study:

- *Does the small size of the initial population of breeding individuals pose a problem for genetic diversity in the Laysan duck? Why or why not?*

- *Is there any aspect of the Laysan duck habitat that may help increase genetic variation in the species and aid in its recovery?*

You need to write a report that answers these two questions and will need to draw on your understanding of evolution to address the species' prospects for long-term recovery. You'll also need to incorporate some information about the Laysan duck's ecology, which includes the following:

- *The Midway Atoll is an isolated island, 2.4 square miles, part of a chain of volcanic islands in the Pacific Ocean.*
- *It is home to 18 different species of bird (2–3 million individuals) that nest on almost every available square foot of the island.*
- *There are no natural predators on the island to threaten the adult birds, but the eggs can fall prey to rats.*
- *Because the Midway Atoll does attract tourists, there are problems with pollution, especially plastic debris that can kill the birds if they ingest it.*

Write your report to your superiors at the U.S. Fish and Wildlife Service. Note that you do not need to use every piece of information provided above. You can pick certain facts and use them as a basis for speculation about the future of the Laysan duck.

The value of this process is that it creates a common framework to both design and review performance assessments so that both the quality of the design work and the capacity of the students to do this work improve. Staff were able to give feedback to one another on the creation of a task without foisting their own preferences on the designer or making the designer feel personally affronted by the advice.

Authenticity in a High School Academy

The next example comes from a consulting project with the staff from a high school law and government academy. The goal was to identify essential 21st century skills that would address the theme of their magnet school and prepare students for postsecondary success.

Key Skills That Run Through Academy Tasks
Ability to

- *Pose and respond to pointed questions.*
- *Conduct oneself in a professional, intelligent manner: etiquette, appropriate language, technical vocabulary.*
- *Calculate budget: estimate costs, propose ways to finance, and execute/revisit plan.*
- *Collaborate with others to complete an assigned task.*
- *Analyze range of sources/points of view to identify bias, logic in order to develop informed opinion.*
- *Use evidence (information, data, statistics, salient quotations) to support thinking.*
- *Develop an idea/position and advocate for it through the development of texts (written, visual, oral, multimedia).*
- *Select appropriate language, techniques, processes, tools, and/or media that communicate the desired message and capture others' attention.*
- *Think "outside of the box"—agile, innovative approaches to a given problem.*
- *Make connections to current events at the local, national, and global levels.*
- *Deliver a professional/publishable presentation.*
- *Research a topic to gain background knowledge—ability to select pertinent information.*
- *Collect data, analyze to determine patterns/trends, display appropriately so that decisions can be made.*
- *Use key technology tools (software, hardware) to communicate with others.*

It took the staff less than two hours to draft these skills and to achieve consensus. What proved much more difficult was determining how to embed them into the design of summative assessments. While the desirability of these skills was apparent to participants during the articulation process, they turned out to be tangential or missing from most of the major assessments that students had been asked to complete. The next step, then, was for us to identify or create new tasks that bridged the worlds of school and life in a 21st century world that will both motivate students and provide means to measure their achievement. Figure 4.1 lists several tasks developed by the academy staff.

Figure 4.1	Law and Government Academy Tasks
The Cost of Living	
Task Summary	Students will work in small groups to quantify specific programs, policies, or life-changing events. The goal is to determine the true costs and reasonable estimates in order to make informed decisions about current and future behavior. Collaboration on this task is critical because of the range in students' prior mathematical knowledge and life experience. In addition, there are multiple solution paths to these open-ended questions that can be developed to calculate/estimate the costs to make sense of the situation.
Academy Skills	• Collaborate with others to complete an assigned task • Collect data, analyze to determine patterns/trends, display appropriately so that decisions can be made • Calculate budget: estimate costs, propose ways to finance, and execute/revisit plan • Use evidence to support thinking • Select appropriate language, techniques, processes, tools, and/or media that communicate the desired message and capture others' attention
Interview (Student as Interviewee)	
Task Summary	Students will market themselves or their ideas in order to achieve a given goal (admission into a program, employment, scholarship, funding, public support). The student is first expected to research the interviewer and organization so that the supporting documents (resume, portfolio, multimedia clips) and verbal responses are appropriate and professional. During the interview process, the student strategically shares information and anecdotes to illustrate strengths and potential contributions that will benefit both the student (or the organization the student represents) and the organization. In addition, students are expected to embody professionalism through their physical appearance, body language, choice of words, and sincerity.
Academy Skills	• Research a topic to gain background knowledge—ability to select pertinent information • Deliver a professional/publishable presentation • Conduct oneself in a professional, intelligent manner: etiquette, appropriate language, technical vocabulary • Pose and respond to pointed questions • Use evidence to support thinking

continued

Figure 4.1	**Law and Government Academy Tasks** (*continued*)
	**Interview (Student as Interviewer)**
Task Summary	Students will conduct an interview in order to elicit information from the subject to achieve a desired result (e.g., deepen knowledge, determine guilt, make decisions). This task requires extensive preparation in order to develop appropriate questions and questioning techniques that will serve as the foundation of the interview. In addition, students are expected to demonstrate effective listening/observational skills and agility through the spontaneous creation of questions based on the responses they are receiving during the experience. After the interview, the student analyzes the information provided to effect the desired result.
Academy Skills	• Research a topic to gain background knowledge—ability to select pertinent information • Analyze range of sources/points of view (interview subject) to identify bias, logic in order to develop informed opinion • Pose and respond to pointed questions • Conduct oneself in a professional, intelligent manner: etiquette, appropriate language, technical vocabulary
	**Community Beautification**
Task Summary	Students will collaborate to develop and execute an idea that will contribute to the aesthetic beauty and health of a place/community. This development process includes surveying the area/neighborhood to determine current condition, interviewing people who live in/use the space to find out their concerns and ideas, proposing and getting approval for the project, developing a plan of action, and completing the task. Technology is expected to be used in order to collect data, effectively document the process, solicit volunteers/contributions, and/or advocate for the project's significance.
Academy Skills	• Collaborate with others to complete an assigned task • Collect data, analyze to determine patterns/trends, display appropriately so that decisions can be made • Analyze range of sources/points of view to identify bias, logic in order to develop informed opinion • Think "outside of the box"—agile, innovative approaches to a given problem • Develop an idea/position and advocate for it through the development of texts • Select appropriate language, techniques, processes, tools, and/or media that communicate the desired message and capture others' attention

	• Calculate budget: estimate costs, propose ways to finance, and execute/revisit plan • Use key technology tools (software, hardware) to communicate with others
Advocacy for a Position	
Task Summary	Students will take a stand on a given issue/problem/proposal based upon critical review of materials as well as prior knowledge and personal experience. In advocating for their position, students will use evidence to support their thinking and address flaws in other points of view. The presentation of their point of view must be persuasive but also respectful in both the articulation of information and the response to questions.
Academy Skills	• Analyze range of sources/points of view to identify bias, logic in order to develop informed opinion • Develop an idea/position and advocate for it through the development of texts • Use evidence to support thinking • Select appropriate language, techniques, processes, tools, and/or media that communicate the desired message and capture others' attention • Pose and respond to pointed questions • Conduct oneself in a professional, intelligent manner: etiquette, appropriate language, technical vocabulary

Source: Law and Government Academy at Hartford Public School. Reprinted by permission.

The authentic messiness and rigor of these tasks require students to intensify their focus and become truly immersed in the work. Not only will these challenges result in improved performance, but they also provide students with the powerful opportunity to enjoy learning in the present moment and discover the relevance of their schoolwork.

Authenticity in Grades K–12 Science

Another approach to improve the authenticity of assessments and coherence of assessment design is to articulate the range of possible tasks that professionals "do" in the field. After collecting possibilities, teachers examine existing assessments to identify what type of task they are and/or revise the task directions and scoring tools to boost authenticity. Science staff in a school district in Texas worked together to delineate the assessment vehicles that scientists use as part of their inquiry and communication of findings. Prior to this work, they had typically written "lab" in their unit plans as an authentic assessment. However, it was abundantly clear to all of the participants that not all labs were equal in cognitive demand or authenticity expected. They established three types of inquiry tasks that reflect these differences (see Figure 4.2).

Figure 4.2	Types of Inquiry Tasks	
Science Assessment Vehicles		**Links to Enduring Understandings**
Procedural Task (Limited Inquiry) Significant parameters (step-by-step instructions, procedures) are provided so that students can demonstrate performance of a targeted skill and/or process. No student inquiry required. • (Elem.) Measure the length of different objects using string and a ruler. • (M.S.) Learn to use a microscope by looking at slides with animal and plant cells. • (H.S.) Learn to use a temperature probe to measure the temperature change in a chemical reaction.		• The terminology used in science has precise meanings both in the investigation and communication of scientific phenomena. • The way scientists conduct an investigation affects its safety, accuracy, precision, reliability, and reproducibility.
Guided Inquiry Task and Accompanying Lab Report With some parameters (i.e., students are given problem and hypothesis; students are given a limited set of materials and equipment), students conduct an investigation that may have multiple paths to a solution or multiple solutions. • (Elem.) Conduct an investigation to determine the effects saltwater solutions have on seed germination. • (M.S.) Conduct an investigation to determine the impact of mechanical weathering on sedimentary rock. • (H.S.) Conduct an investigation to determine how different surfaces affect the velocity of a toy car.		• Scientific inquiry is a thoughtful and coordinated attempt to search out, describe, explain, and predict natural phenomena. • By varying just one condition at a time, scientists can hope to identify its exclusive effects on what happens. • The way scientists conduct an investigation affects its safety, accuracy, precision, reliability, and reproducibility. • Graphs, tables, and charts provide visual representations that allow scientists to see the relationship between variables. • The terminology used in science has precise meanings both in the investigation and communication of scientific phenomena.

Full Inquiry Task and Accompanying Lab Report Student independently designs an investigation that has multiple paths to a solution or multiple solutions.	• Scientific inquiry is a thoughtful and coordinated attempt to search out, describe, explain, and predict natural phenomena.
• (Elem.) Design a humdinger that hums when you pull the string and dings when you release the string. • (M.S.) Design and conduct an experiment about a more expeditious way to compost organic matter. • (H.S.) Design an experiment to determine how heat affects the properties of a solid.	• Generating and testing hypotheses is the method by which scientists learn about the universe. • By varying just one condition at a time, scientists can hope to identify its exclusive effects on what happens. • The way scientists conduct an investigation affects its safety, accuracy, precision, reliability, and reproducibility. • Graphs, tables, and charts provide visual representations that allow scientists to see the relationship between variables. • The terminology used in science has precise meanings both in the investigation and communication of scientific phenomena.

Source: Carrollton-Farmers Branch Independent School District. Reprinted by permission.

Immediately after these examples were articulated, a participant asked, "Do we have to do all three types of inquiry tasks? I don't know who, if anyone, has students do full inquiry tasks." I replied to the group, asking, "Is it reasonable that as part of their PreK–12 science education students have at least two to three opportunities to do this work?"

Another participant responded, "Well, of course. That's what science is." Then the first participant asked, "But how do we find the time to do that kind of science with everything else we have to do?" There was a long pause, then: "I guess I just answered my own question! We have to find time in the curriculum to do science." Participants then went on the hunt for meaningful places to build in full inquiry tasks. This exchange reveals the expeditious assessment "ruts" we have developed in lieu of keeping in mind the more robust learning goals that are fundamental to the discipline. Interestingly enough, many state standards documents have been revised in recent years to reflect these more global aims.

A Shared Definition of Quality

Authentic tasks require the creation of scoring tools that place appropriate emphasis on quality of thinking, the ability to execute the task, and the effectiveness of the result. It is important to teach our learners that grades are not personal, but a description of their current achievement. When we provide learners with candid feedback based on an established and consistent set of criteria, they can focus on what they can do to improve their work instead of trying to "work the system" or hope the rules change to curry more success. Therefore, scoring tools and grading policies should not be impersonal as well. Rubrics should be collectively developed and adopted by classroom teachers so that learners trust that their performance is driven by the nature of the discipline, not the personal preferences of the teacher.

A school district in Virginia developed an impressive collection of rubrics to evaluate 21st century skills. The premise was that if these skills were measured on a K–12 continuum, then teachers would work to embed them in a meaningful way in assessment design and grading and reporting systems. An excerpt from their continuum can be found in Figure 4.3.

This continuum was developed by a heavyweight team (see Chapter 3) composed of individuals who represented a range of expertise in curriculum content, knowledge of diversity of learners, and expectations for postsecondary success. This mix of curriculum specialists, school leaders, and community members devoted four full days to craft language that was coherent, multidisciplinary, and ambitious. Once the design task was completed, the team disbanded and the work became the responsibility of existing middleweight teams (curriculum content area teachers, division leadership teams, school faculties) to determine what existing tasks would provide evidence of student learning on the continua and to develop new tasks that would provide additional evidence and opportunity to learn.

Figure 4.3	Excerpt from a Rubric to Evaluate 21st Century Skills			
21st Century Skill	Novice	Emerging	Proficient	Advanced
Collaboration: *Interact with diverse groups to achieve an objective while displaying flexibility and willingness to understand alternate points of view.*	Shares information and ideas with others to complete a given task.	Expresses own ideas and appropriately responds to diverse points of view in order to create a shared plan of action to solve a problem or complete a given task.	Assumes shared responsibility for the creation of a unified product or proposed solution through the exploration of a range of ideas, establishment of a collective plan of action, and completion of individual responsibilities.	Networks locally and remotely with diverse peers, experts, and others to leverage collective expertise in the design and execution of an effective plan of action to solve a complex problem or complete an interdependent task.
Sustainability: *Foster responsible development and protection of the world's natural environment and resources through individual and collective action.*	Takes actions to maintain and improve the health of an environment based on information, prompts, and good citizenship.	Demonstrates basic understanding of the impact of human behaviors and natural phenomena on the environment through examination of data and personal actions.	Analyzes consumption patterns, energy sources, and economic factors to determine how individuals, companies, and governments work to improve the health of an environment for future generations and uses that analysis to create a compelling vision for collective action.	Applies knowledge of the dynamic interdependence of economic, environmental, and societal factors to research and develop new ideas/products that will impact consumption patterns and improve environmental conditions.
Health Literacy: *Make informed decisions based on appropriate sources for a healthy lifestyle.*	Identifies healthy choices and engages in healthy behaviors based on information, prompts, and examples provided by external sources.	Selects strategies based on self-awareness and knowledge of healthy practices that promote physical and emotional well-being.	Evaluates the impact of choices on personal well-being based on self-awareness, life experience, and scientific knowledge to inform decision making.	Makes deliberate adjustments to personal behaviors based on current health, self-awareness, external factors, intrinsic motivation, and newly acquired knowledge to promote well-being and a healthy lifestyle.

Source: Virginia Beach City Public Schools. Reprinted by permission.

Record of Accomplishment

While a high school diploma and transcript indicate the completion of necessary course credits and examinations, they do not provide learners (or their future employers) with clarity about what students accomplished during their time in school. Perhaps one of the most powerful but most overlooked components of authentic assessment is the documentation of student work in portfolios. Portfolios have had moments of popularity (most notably in the areas of English language arts and visual arts); ideally, they comprise a collection of a learner's work throughout his or her time in school demonstrating the achievement of mission-driven goals. The collection should include both required tasks designed by the teacher and self-generated tasks pursued out of genuine interest, curiosity, and passion.

Recent improvements in the ability of districts to warehouse data and the ability of adults to effectively access electronic information will contribute to the potential power of these records. Imagine if every learner led an annual conference with teachers and parents to explain what pieces best exemplified his or her current achievement (as measured by an established continuum or set of criteria), which was followed by a strategy session identifying what goals, approaches, and opportunities would best support the learner's continued growth in the following school year. This conference could take place as a physical meeting or a virtual discussion to provide periodic updates based on new work completed and to review the effectiveness of personalized plans. This collection of work would also provide valuable information to potential employers, admissions officers, coaches, and mentors about a learner's demonstrated achievement.

Encouraging Students to Struggle

For authentic tasks to motivate our learners, students must come to accept those tasks as challenging, achievable, and worthy of the attempt. The challenge of the task comes from requiring something deeper than a memory-based response. Learners must apply what they already know, are able to do, and understand to make sense of an unfamiliar or daunting situation. It should be explicitly clear to everyone in the classroom that there will be no speedy answers, no instant gratification, and no quick fixes. Teachers should openly discuss the frustration, obstacles, and roadblocks that are to be expected and embraced.

Nevertheless, it is important that the task be achievable, and carefully designed by staff so that students have the appropriate space to succeed. Rubrics and exemplars should communicate clear expectations about what quality looks like, informing the development, reflection, and revision of work. Learners should receive feedback about their work based on rubric criteria that provide them with clarity needed to improve performance. Teachers should emphasize the importance of revision through their grading policies and allocation of time (both within scheduled class time and outside of class).

Finally, the task must be worthy of effort to learners, helping them see the connection between what they are doing and the real world. While they may feel anxious about their ability to be successful, they can trust that their attempts will teach them more about the subject and about themselves. They will also find worth in the notion that what they are doing has the potential to benefit a larger community: their words, ideas, solution paths, data, and products could add value to the lives of others. With authentic tasks, they will experience kinship with other students and professionals in the field who engage in similar tasks and experience similar highs and lows.

Making Learning Enjoyable

Authentic tasks are worth the struggle for students not just because they lay the groundwork for future success, but because they are enjoyable in the present. In order to deeply enjoy an experience, the learner must become immersed in the work. This conception of enjoyment is quite different from pleasure, according to Csikszentmihalyi (1990): "A person can feel pleasure without any effort, if the appropriate centers in his brain are electrically stimulated, or as a result of the chemical stimulation of drugs. But it is impossible to enjoy a tennis game, a book, or a conversation unless attention is fully concentrated on the activity" (p. 46).

It is important to underscore that enjoyment does not supplant intensity or rigor. In fact, quite the opposite is true. Students' immersion in a task results in higher-quality work because they are committed to what they are doing instead of just being committed to getting it finished. Csikszentmihalyi notes, "What counts is to set a goal, to concentrate one's psychic energy, to pay attention to feedback, and to make certain that the challenge is appropriate to one's skill. Sooner or later the interaction will begin to hum, and the flow experience follows" (pp. 190–191). Enjoyment is absolutely intrinsic—it cannot be invoked by a gold star, a report card grade, or a pizza party.

Emphasis on Creativity in Task Design

In addition to the characteristics explored above, student tasks are made more engaging when we infuse them with a need for creativity, which enhances quality of thought, problem solving, and skill development in the classroom. The justification for working to include creativity in our assignments is grounded in three key facts:

- Creativity depends upon a strong knowledge base and ongoing rigorous skill development.
- Creativity is quantified through research as a predictable process.
- Creativity is developed through habit.

While creativity is only one of the established 21st century skills (think back to Chapter 2), it is often the most undervalued or marginalized in school curricula. Educators and policymakers have primarily delegated creativity to the fine arts (which students may engage in for as little as 20 minutes per week) and to a handful of grade-level expectations in English language arts. The more robust definitions of creativity come from 21st century skills initiatives. Figure 4.4 shows the way the Partnership for 21st Century Skills (2009) incorporates the definition of creativity and innovation as part of its learning framework. Upon reading definitions like this one, many educators struggle to figure out how to engage students in this type of thinking and working. Not only are there other curricular and assessment priorities, but educators also are genuinely confused about how to develop creativity within their subject-area coursework.

Figure 4.4	P21 Framework Definition of Creativity
Think Creatively	**Work Creatively with Others**
• Use a wide range of idea creation techniques (such as brainstorming) • Create new and worthwhile ideas (both incremental and radical concepts) • Elaborate, refine, analyze and evaluate their own ideas in order to improve and maximize creative efforts	• Develop, implement and communicate new ideas to others effectively • Be open and responsive to new and diverse perspectives; incorporate group input and feedback into the work • Demonstrate originality and inventiveness in work and understand the real world limits to adopting new ideas • View failure as an opportunity to learn; understand that creativity and innovation is a long-term, cyclical process of small successes and frequent mistakes

Source: From "P21 Framework Definitions," by Partnership for 21st Century Skills, 2009. Available online: www.p21.org/documents/P21_Framework_Definitions.pdf. Reprinted by permission.

To address this confusion, let's begin with a basic working definition of creativity. Sir Ken Robinson (2006) suggests a simple but powerful one: "the process of having original ideas that have value." These ideas are generated by the learner as a result of the connections they create, often through capturing information, ideas, and flashes of insight.

Grounded in Knowledge

Many children and adults alike underestimate the role of skill and hard work in the development of creativity. The "greats" in sports, science, the arts, and business are viewed by many as mythological legends who are able to see and do what is impossible to mere mortals. Carol Dweck (2006) points to classic childhood stories that perpetuate this notion that effort is what the less capable resort to because they lack natural ability:

> The story of the tortoise and the hare, in trying to put forward the power of effort, gave effort a bad name. It reinforced the image that effort is for plodders and suggested that in rare instances, when talented people dropped the ball, the plodder could sneak through. The little engine that could, the saggy, baggy elephant, and the scruffy tugboat—they were cute, they were often overmatched, and we were happy for them when they succeeded. . . . The problem was that these stories made it into an either-or. Either you have ability or you expend effort. And this is part of the fixed mindset. Effort is for those who don't have the ability. People with the fixed mindset tell us, "If you have to work at something, you must not be good at it." They add, "Things come easily to people who are true geniuses." (pp. 39–40)

The truth is much less fanciful. While some are born endowed with great capacities, all humans are natural learners who have the capacity for creativity and intelligence. Consider the joy so many young children experience when they are given the opportunity to paint. They imagine vivid stories in their heads that take form on the paper. They use their brushes, their fingers, their colors to bring those ideas to life. They are fearless. And then one day, many of them change. They become reluctant to pick up a paintbrush, worried when what is in their heads doesn't "look right" on paper, fearful that their work does not measure up to that of other students. They often decide that they are not artists and stop engaging in the production. Creativity requires the innocence and/or tenacity to remain fearless so that the mind remains open to an array of possibilities.

Creativity also requires the commitment to mastering key skills, procedures, and terminology that are the basis of a discipline. Teachers must openly challenge the misconception that creativity falls out of the sky or is accessible only to a select few. This point is critical to improving the receptivity of teachers, students, and parents to including creativity instruction in the curriculum. Following are several quotations that speak to the need to study the work of creativity "masters" intensively as a foundation for one's own creative developments.

> It is a mistake to assume that creativity and rote learning are incompatible. Some of the most original scientists, for instance, have been known to have memorized music, poetry, or historical information extensively. (Csikszentmihalyi, 1990, p. 123)

Mozart once said, "People err who think my art comes easily to me. I assure you, dear friend, nobody has devoted so much time and thought to composition as I. There is not a famous master whose music I have not studied many times." (Tharp, 2003, pp. 8–9)

These notions about creativity, espoused by great artists and scientists, are also supported by neuroscientists. When learners work until the point that a skill becomes automatic and knowledge is instantly accessible, working memory is freed up to think about more interesting ideas. Here are two key scientific findings put forth by Daniel Willingham (2009) about the necessity of acquisition of knowledge and practice of skill in order to become more advanced:

> You practice not only to get faster. What's important is getting so good that [it] becomes automatic. If it's automatic you have freed working-memory space . . . that can now be devoted to thinking about meaning. (p. 87)

> All of the information in long-term memory resides outside of awareness. It lies quietly until needed, and then enters working memory so it becomes conscious. . . . Thinking occurs when you combine information (from the environment and long-term memory) in new ways. That combining happens in working memory. (p. 11)

While deep knowledge and fluent skills are vital to learning, they are not the ultimate goal of one's education. The purpose of deep study and diligent practice is to cultivate one's own ideas—to be able to apply learning to make sense of new problems, challenges, and inquiries. The challenge comes in determining how to balance learners' need to engage in deep study and practice with their need to "play" and apply what they have learned through creative problem solving and expression.

The Four-Step Process of Creativity

Creativity appears to be an amorphous concept to many, but the elements of the creative thinking process are actually quite consistently documented in both research and in autobiographical and biographical descriptions of accomplished creative individuals in their respective fields. To delve deeper into the nature of creativity, it is useful to break it down into its component parts:

Many researchers see creative thinking as a four-step process: preparation, incubation, illumination and verification or revision. Preparation is consciously studying a task, and perhaps trying to attack it logically by standard means. Incubation, the "mystical" step, is one in which both the conscious mind and the subconscious mull over the problem in hard-to-define ways. Illumination, the "Eureka!" step, is seeing a new synthesis; and verification and revision include all the work that comes after. (Florida, 2004, p. 33)

These four steps are explored in more detail below through a deliberate pairing of two very different authorities on the subject: Dr. Robert Epstein, a prominent researcher on creativity, and Twyla Tharp, a renowned choreographer. The intent of the pairing is to model how fresh thoughts arise when we broaden the scope of our inquiry beyond current areas of expertise.

Preparation

Creativity requires seeking out knowledge through deliberate actions as well as being open to intuitive ones. While there may be a defined task to complete with an expected deadline, the preparation phase can be unpredictable as an individual begins to discover the nature of the problem. A key challenge for the individual is to develop a plan or process that provides some structure for the endeavor while remaining receptive to new ideas and directions. According to Tharp,

Your creative endeavors can never be thoroughly mapped out ahead of time. You have to allow for the suddenly altered landscape, the change in plan, the accidental spark—and you have to see it as a stroke of luck rather than a disturbance of your perfect scheme. Habitually creative people are, in E. B. White's phrase, "prepared to be lucky." . . . Remaining open to "fresh thoughts" is vital as many new imaginings can become inflexible. It's tempting to try to rein in the unruliness of the creative process, especially at the start. Planning lets you impose order on the chaotic process of making something new, but when it's taken too far you get locked into a status quo, and creative thinking is about breaking free from the status quo, even one you made yourself. That's why it's vital to know the difference between good planning and too much planning. (2003, pp. 120–122)

Preparation, then, requires the opportunity to inhabit a problem and make sense of it. The work involves practicing existing skills, acquiring new knowledge, capturing snippets of ideas (whether partially developed, random, or vividly apparent), developing and following a direction, and investing the effort to get ready to "get lucky."

Incubation

Incubation requires the space to play with ideas and sit with questions without worrying about the quality or reception of the end result. Space is multidimensional here—it is the emotional space to think without fear or self-doubt tearing down new ideas; it is the time to think without deadlines (arbitrary or actual) determining when the work is to be done; it is the physical space to think that provides comfort, structure, and inspiration to do one's best work; and it is the space in time where one lives that connects the present attempt to the deep knowledge of the masters that have come before this and the imagining of the greatness yet to come. Consider the following description of how Beethoven developed his ideas for musical compositions:

> Beethoven, despite his unruly reputation and his wild romantic image, was well organized. He saved everything in a series of notebooks that were organized according to the level of development of the idea. He had notebooks for rough ideas, notebooks for improvements on those ideas, and notebooks for finished ideas, almost as if he was pre-aware of an idea's early, middle and late stages. . . . He might take an original three-note motif and push it to its next stage by dropping one of the notes a half tone and doubling it. Then he'd let the idea sit there for another six months. It would reappear in a third notebook, again not copied but further improved, perhaps inverted this time and ready to be used in a piano sonata. He never puts the ideas back exactly the same. He always moves them forward, and by doing so, he re-energizes them. (Tharp, 2003, p. 83)

During this phase, the individual seeks new connections from an overwhelming array of thoughts, ideas, and sketches. The construction of these connections provides the possibility for breakthroughs in our knowledge of the world, our ability to tell a story, our development of a new product, and our capacity to empathize with others.

While the possibilities may generate excitement, this phase also can feel painful. Stress, anxiety, fear, and confusion can depress the individual who has invested tremendous attention and time into an endeavor that remains elusive. Neurologically, we are in fact "overloaded" as we work to create new meaning. Epstein elaborates:

> According to Generativity Theory, novel behavior (including the verbal and perceptual behaviors we often call "ideas") is the result of an orderly and dynamic competition among previously established behaviors, during which old behaviors blend or become interconnected in new ways. . . . The computational complexity of the process alone is probably enough to make it seem mysterious. New ideas often seem to come out of the blue, mainly because we cannot track the antecedent events or processes. (1999, p. 763)

Emotionally, we become worried that the combinatory play won't materialize, won't work, won't be well received, won't be worthy. Fears, cynicism, and self-doubt can halt the creative process because individuals give up too soon or worry too much about how others will judge them and their work. This phase requires tolerance for unpredictable paths, unexpected roadblocks, and unfortunate delays. Amid all of this cognitive and emotive frustration, there is a perceptible sense that the solution is almost within reach—that we have somehow gotten closer to what we have been searching for all along.

Illumination

The mystical component of creativity appears in the illumination phase. From seemingly out of nowhere, the solution, formula, phrasing, story, composition, or idea appears and the work and the individual are forever changed. Notable authors describe being "taken over" by the story as they create, as if the fictional characters use them as a medium. Notable musicians describe hearing the composition in their head and working feverishly to capture the fully realized sound as it plays in their minds. For a window in time, something has become unlocked in the mind of the creator that reveals truth, beauty, opportunity, and/or the powers of the universe. Knowing that this moment of illumination is possible drives the creator to remain vigilant in his or her expansion and refinement of skills and playful with the exploration of new ideas and materials, so that when the moment reveals itself, it is possible to capture it.

Verification and Revision

This final phase of creative work requires meticulous execution of the creative conception so that it can have the desired impact. The refinement of the product, reworking of the text, modification of the strategy, or adaptation of the original idea requires as much tenacity, skill, and perseverance as was demonstrated before the illumination phase. Elation with the concept can be overwhelmed by real obstacles in the production of the work and communication to a larger audience. Just because an individual figured something out does not mean that the rest of the world is prepared for it. In addition to honing the final product, the individual must also be prepared to defend, explain, and contextualize the evolution of the work so that it is more likely to be understood. The intent is not to justify the effort, but to clarify the value of this new synthesis of information and ideas. Ultimately, the worthiness of the work is not measured by accolades or financial rewards but by whether the creator believes that the work was meaningful.

Moving to Action

Now that the steps in the process of creativity have been established, it is appropriate to consider how to embed this progression into all levels of the learning organization.

What Can One Teacher Do?

While all individuals have the capacity for creativity, it must be cultivated through the thinking we engage in and the time we commit to the work. Art Costa (2008) explains:

> Like strenuous movement, skillful thinking is hard work. And as with athletics, students need practice, reflection, and coaching to think well. With proper instruction, human thought processes can become more broadly applied, more spontaneously generated, more precisely focused, more complex and more insightfully divergent. (p. 21)

Let's look at four competencies of creativity (based on the research of Robert Epstein) in light of learning how to meet the challenge of embedding creativity into the daily work of the classroom: capturing,

challenging, broadening, and surrounding. By translating these competencies into instructional habits, teachers can more consistently provide
students with meaningful opportunities to play with ideas and produce
original works.

The first instructional habit to encourage creativity in the classroom
is to train students to capture their thinking. Whether they use a box, a
sketchbook, a journal, or a collection of scrap papers, the habit of capturing puts students in the fascinating pursuit of engaging in work with
no established purpose, deadline, or format. Far from being a waste of
time, this eclectic collection becomes a constant source of inspiration
for students in their own writing, experiments, and solution paths.
They learn to tinker with their thinking, adjust their perspective, and
hone their use of language because they are intrinsically motivated by
the power of the idea. The first habit is the easiest to implement—ideas
are everywhere once we become attuned to noticing them when they
show up. Train students to notice them by creating a formal capturing
time in the class period as well as a designated repository for their ideas
(notebook, file folder, etc.). In addition, openly encourage students
to add to this repository whenever inspiration strikes so that they can
then resume focus on the task at hand. This collection does not need
to be formally graded or evaluated. Instead, it provides a rich context
for teacher-student conferences as well as a treasure trove of ideas for
teachers and students to develop projects that provide the opportunity
to explore an idea more deeply.

The second instructional habit is the creation of challenging problems for students to contemplate that push them beyond what they
already know how to do. Epstein (2010) describes the importance of
taking on such open-ended challenges. Teachers not only need to design
problems that push students beyond their comfort zone, but also must
teach students how to stay "stuck" for a while instead of giving up,
looking for someone to do the thinking for them, or misinterpreting
the struggle as a sign of stupidity.

Again, it is vital that students become acclimated to struggle as a sign
of learning instead of a sign of weakness. Creative people view failure
as important feedback in the development of their ideas. This does not
make failure more pleasurable, but rather an unavoidable aspect of the

endeavor. Twyla Tharp explains, "Failure creates an interesting tug of war between forgetting and remembering. It's vital to be able to forget the pain of failure while retaining the lessons from it" (2003, p. 214). Many teachers (and parents) flinch at the notion of students failing. Schools have become so averse to failure that they have attempted to scaffold learning to the point where failure is not an option. Problems are likely to have answers and set solution paths. Research assignments are likely to have a set structure to steer how and what students explore. Communication tasks have specific directions about format and content. Revision opportunities are about fixing errors more than understanding the nature of them. We reinforce a fixed mind-set in our learners because we don't have the time or intestinal fortitude to do otherwise. Instead, as teachers, we should re-instill the "childlike fearlessness" students possessed when they were younger and more keen on exploration of the unknown. Epstein (1999) contends that students are in fact most creative in their kindergarten year, and that by the end of 1st grade they have had their creativity socialized out of them by the demands of the curriculum. An important part of the instructional habit of challenging students, then, is creating the space for them to struggle. That means that the problem or question will endure regardless of students' desire to dismiss it and move on. It also means that the way we evaluate student work must be based on the knowledge they construct and the connections they develop, instead of the amount of time it takes to solve a problem or whether they arrive at a predictable result.

The third instructional habit is broadening one's existing knowledge base to seek out new areas—the more uncharacteristic for the learner, the better. The value of breaking down boundaries between disciplines has become popularized in business literature by Frans Johansson (2004), author of *The Medici Effect*. Johansson contends that the discoveries that will change the world will come from the combinatory play of seemingly disparate fields of study. Consider the following illustration, posted by Frans Johansson on the Medici Effect blog on February 22, 2009 (www.themedicieffect.com/2009/02):

> Volvo has delved into a new, fascinating, and intersectional initiative. The car company's vision is to develop a collision safety system for automobiles based on the African grasshopper's ability to not collide when it

flies in swarms. . . . Jonas Ekmark, preventive safety leader at Volvo Safety Division, points out how amazing it is that these grasshoppers can fly around in a chaotic swarm, looking for food, yet never once collide with each other. He feels that the discovery about the locust's radar system has the potential of yielding information that could be used to develop new technology to cut down on road traffic accidents.

The connection between the locust's sensory system and a potential road traffic safety system was made by Dr. Claire Rind at Newcastle University, in the UK. When asked how she came up with it, she answers that she thinks it came from her own experience as a driver and a pedestrian. . . . The Volvo safety division heard about Dr. Rind's research, and thought it could be of use particularly in regard to pedestrian safety. The automobile company hopes to reproduce the locust's radar system onto a computer chip, and install it inside a camera, which would compose the car's safety system—although, so far, current hardware and software systems have proved unable to replicate the locust's sensory system.

The notion of interdisciplinary projects is familiar to many educators. Though appealing in theory, the creation of such designs can overwhelm teachers and students as they try to implement and manage the tasks. It is complicated work to find true interrelationships instead of obvious topic matches. It is also complicated to predict the most fertile opportunities for students, determine who is responsible for students' achievement, re-conceptualize one part of school without causing a ripple effect in the rest of the organizational structure, or find teachers who have the curiosity, passion, and growth mind-set to shift away from the current way of working in pursuit of something amorphous. Despite these and dozens more complications (funding, facilities, urgency to improve test scores, and so forth), the fact remains that the creative combination of diverse fields, peoples, and cultures engenders fascinating results.

There are ways to embrace broadening as a habit without restructuring the design of school. For example, students can research fields of study (majors in college, research and development projects at companies, new careers) that didn't exist 10 years ago to determine how those branches of thinking emerged and learn about the aspirations of individuals engaged in the work. Students also can listen to TED Talks, a powerful collection of more than 450 speeches lasting 18 minutes or less by "the world's most inspired thinkers." TED Talks are designed to allow these experts to share their specific area of expertise with a diverse audience. The talks are available online at the TED Web site (www.ted .com) and are sure to intrigue teachers and students alike about new areas of knowledge. Students also can be given access to experts within their own community via robust extracurricular offerings and specially scheduled events or blocks of time. A monthly guest speaker program could provide a valuable opportunity to learn from community members; a "special activity" block could provide staff with the opportunity to offer mini-courses in their individual areas of expertise, academic or otherwise (hobbies, culture, etc.). It is amazing how diverse these mini-courses can be and how passion can spread to the work within regular class periods.

Of course, those educators who truly want to broaden learning for students could tear down the walls that separate the disciplines and create more interdisciplinary learning environments centered around student inquiry, exploration, and communication. The projects students would pursue would become the guide for developing the requisite skills and the areas of knowledge they chose to explore. In a standards-based, test-driven world, broadening to this extent seems next to impossible. For those who have the courage to disrupt their organization, though, there are schools that have embraced this approach and that can provide powerful models, such as High Tech High School in California (http://hightechhigh.org) and Big Picture Schools in Rhode Island (www.bigpicture.org/schools). Both schools center their integrated curriculum programs around inquiry, authentic tasks, and problem solving. The constant of their curricular programs is learning how to learn, how to collaborate, how to access information, how to reason, and how to communicate. The knowledge base itself can be as fluid as the interests of the students.

The fourth and final instructional habit is "surrounding." Epstein's (1999) research reveals that changing a static learning environment can stimulate creativity: "The individual changes his or her physical and social environments on a regular basis. Resurgence gets multiple repertoires competing, and so do unusual or diverse environments" (p. 765). Many individuals develop patterns in how they think and work that unintentionally inhibit fresh thoughts. They tend to gravitate toward peers and colleagues who have similar preferences and world-views. They tend to sit in the same location during meetings. They tend to follow similar processes for the development of a task. They tend to expect a similar result, commensurate with previous efforts. Shaking up this constancy produces the disequilibrium necessary to see things in a new light. As simplistic as it sounds, try asking participants who are developing a plan of action, working to make sense of a difficult problem, or drafting a concept to stand up and change their seats partway through the meeting. When I pull this stunt, many participants openly resist relocation because they are comfortable with where they are. After their initial annoyance subsides, participants resume their work, but the dynamic shifts. The collaboration that ensues is fed through large-group exchanges as well as by exchanges between participants sitting next to each other.

Another strategy is to bring new materials for participants to play with and explore without any expectation of implementing them. The goal is for them to explore possibilities and inspire one another with their imaginings and connections. For example, if I purchased a class set of pocket-sized video cameras (now available for approximately $50), what would students be able to create? How might the cameras inspire their thinking? What impact might they have on the school community? On the world? Some educators dismiss such fanciful thinking because of a lack of money, time, energy, faith in students to care for the equipment, and so on. Whether the class set of video cameras materializes or not is not the point—what is relevant is the ability to consider how a potential change in the way we work could revolutionize our notion of what is possible.

A third strategy for surrounding is to learn about how and what students learn in schools around the city, country, and world. For example, there is a primary school in Australia that demonstrates how to change the world in five minutes a day through their class projects on topics such as recycling old cell phones and cultivating a school vegetable garden; videos of their projects can be found online. Students could also compare the education practices, policies, and curricula of the nations whose schools score in the top five places on the Programme for International Student Assessment (PISA) to practices in the United States to seek good ideas for how to make schools work better for students. A final example is to watch *Two Million Minutes,* a documentary about how students around the world spend their time between the end of eighth grade and their high school graduation and what effect their choices have on the trajectory of their lives.

What Can One Department or Program Do?

Colleagues can collaborate to identify contemporary developments in their respective fields that drive new research studies, new interdisciplinary niches, new products, and new forms of expression. As part of this work, staff will become well-versed in changes in working conditions, technology tools, and future directions. They can use this knowledge in turn to inspire the design of authentic tasks as well as to seek out partnerships with professionals in their field who could use the assistance of their students. They can also use this information to reframe existing course or grade-level curricula, as well as propose new areas of focus. Keep in mind the point made at the beginning of the discussion: creativity must remain grounded in knowledge and skill development. Therefore, it is imperative that curricular documents be thoroughly reviewed for an appropriate balance of preparation and creativity and ample space for students to engage in the four-step process. Expect that an increased emphasis on creativity will supplant other topics and tasks that currently exist.

What Can One School or School System Do?

For creativity to become a fixture in the classroom, we must also embed it in professional learning. Staff must consistently engage in the exploration and development of new ideas insulated from fear of retribution from other colleagues, fear of losing the support of leadership, and fear of failure (such as a short-term dip in test scores). Consider David Thielen's explanation of how Microsoft manages creativity:

> 1. Hire smart people who think. The company's interview process is designed to separate the people who think from those who simply perform tasks.

2. Expect employees to fail. If you work in an environment in which the best route to job security is by working to outdo the company's competition, you focus your energy on developing new products and new ways to solve problems.

3. Keep repercussions small when conquest-oriented employees make mistakes. If employees don't fail, they're not taking enough risks. In some cases they've even been promoted because of what they learned from their failures.

4. Create an us vs. them mentality. Microsoft employees are constantly reminded that their competition is other companies, not colleagues.

5. Sustain the company's start-up mentality. There's an ever-present sense of urgency that the business must succeed. Make it everyone's responsibility to watch costs.

6. Make the office feel like home. Create a work environment that is as nice or nicer than home, and employees will want to be there. . . . There's a big connection between enjoying your work and doing good work. (Cited in Florida, 2004, p. 131)

What corollaries are there between this set of guidelines and the way we treat staff within our own organizations?

- Do we treat our staff as "smart people who think"? Or do we treat them as cogs in a larger K–12 curricular wheel?
- Do staff fail gloriously when trying something ambitious and/or new and improve based on the experience, or do they avoid failure at all costs?
- Do we create a sense of urgency around finding a way to support every learner, or do we decide success is not possible for some?
- Do we make the school feel like a family, or do staff retreat from the building as quickly as possible?
- Do staff celebrate the accomplishments and successes of other staff, or do they begrudge them the honor?

Staff must become reinvigorated by the possibility that their school can be a true learning organization, not just for students but also for themselves. They must model the courageous pursuit of the unknown, the willingness to develop new capacities even when existing ones seem sufficient, the fascination with areas of expertise outside of their own, and the grace of growing from failure instead of becoming devastated by it.

Leaders can create a research and development committee in their school to explore new opportunities for students to engage in their schoolwork. These fledgling ideas can be shepherded through their development by a handful of enthusiastic staff and students. Staff can create a shared reading library based on a blend of education literature and other genres that inspire their thinking, with a breadth of titles that will inspire a range of new connections. Staff can adopt journaling as a fixture of their professional work to capture new ideas that occur to them in the midst of designing and facilitating learning for students. They can seek feedback from their colleagues based on the inspiration for their ideas as well as how to improve upon them. During part of their assigned meeting or preparation times, staff can create their own pet projects with the potential to improve the quality of learning in the organization. Google management is renowned for its creation of the "20 percent rule," under which employees can spend one day per week working on a project of their own choice. Workers share their special projects with their colleagues, and the most promising ideas are pursued at a larger scale. This trust in the employees to work hard on the company's pursuits for 80 percent of their time and chase small and large dreams during the other 20 percent nourishes the creative, upstart spirit of this powerful company. The percentage of time is not as significant as the sincerity of the intent and the transparent and deep commitment to growing ideas. Whatever directions you pursue or choices you make, know that the work of education is by nature a dynamic, collaborative, creative endeavor that requires the voluntary dedication of staff in order to achieve the desired achievement results.

Conclusion

Learning organizations measure their success by the demonstrated ability of learners to achieve mission-driven goals. Authentic tasks must play a dominant role in an assessment system so that students can experience true rigor in the disciplines they pursue. This chapter reviewed five characteristics of this type of task design as well as the significance of creativity to this work.

An important subtext throughout the chapter has been challenging the nine myths from Chapter 1. You may want to reflect on what you have learned in light of that connection. Can you see how learners would need to rethink those axioms if the nature of the work they were asked to do was more authentic? You may also want to think about the extent to which the content of subsequent chapters has influenced your thinking about the original reflection question.

Original Chapter 1 Reflection Question

Is fundamental change possible given the myths our culture holds related to schooling?

5

Designing Learning Environments That Reflect Our Knowledge of Learning and Our Realization of Mission and Vision

Reflection Question

What is learning most naturally like? How can we open up opportunities for learning in our schools?

There are many topics on which educators are well-versed and quite certain that they know what's best for their students. There are many additional areas of learning that educators actively pursue in order to improve student achievement. One area that would benefit both educators and students if they took the time to explore it in much more depth is the science of learning. We make numerous judgments about who we are as learners: how we best function, what subjects we excel at and where we struggle, and what we think we can handle on our own and where we need help. So much of what we think we know about learning, however, is based on inaccurate or incomplete information.

This chapter delves into the science of learning through a brief review of key research findings and an explanation of the need for establishing learning principles. The idea is simple—if we have better knowledge of how learning happens (regardless of age, achievement gap, gender, race, etc.), then we have both the leverage and responsibility to do what works for learners. This preliminary exploration of research findings is designed to inspire educators and students alike. Knowledge of the brain and how people learn can be transformative, not only in reimagining key routines and structures of school, but also in reinvigorating students' commitment to practicing skills and memorizing essential facts. We will then outline two key actions that a school or school system can take: establishing learning principles about what practices are necessary to optimize learning, and determining what practices do not have the desired effect on learning. The latter half of the chapter focuses on how to further reconnect learners to the learning organization by clarifying the notion of student engagement and tapping into students' search for purpose.

IF we design learning that is respectful and relevant to the learners and consider their prior knowledge, personal experiences, and current needs through

- identifying and promoting instructional practices, structures, and policies that are supported by research;
- ensuring the workload is prioritized, personalized, and manageable;
- developing feedback mechanisms and models of quality work to provide comprehensible information about current performance and ways to improve future performance;
- creating space to focus on an assignment, explain thinking, and reflect on the process;
- creating space to explore alternate solution paths, points of view, tangents, questions, and interdisciplinary connections;
- creating space to struggle without feeling rushed, overanxious, or penalized; and
- creating substantive opportunities to improve students' work . . .

THEN we can engage all learners in the acquisition of key knowledge and skills and the development of connections so that they can pursue powerful questions, tackle complex problems, collaborate with diverse people, imagine new possibilities, and communicate their ideas.

The Science of Learning

Svinicki, Hagen, and Meyer (1996) described learning this way:

> Learning begins with the need for some motivation, an intention to learn. The learner must then concentrate attention on the important aspects of what is to be learned and differentiate them from noise in the environment. While those important aspects are being identified, the learner accesses the prior knowledge that already exists in memory, because a key to learning is connecting what is known to what is being learned. New information must be processed, structured, and connected in such a way as to be accessible in the future; this process is known as encoding. The deeper the processing of the information in terms of its underlying organization, the better the learning and later retrieval of that information. This processing requires active involvement. The learner must verify an understanding of the structure by receiving feedback, from the internal and external environments, on the encoding choices made. (p. 257)

Whether reflecting on this passage on your own or discussing it with colleagues, consider how this research-based explanation of learning might affect classroom-level practice. Here are just a few questions that might emerge:

- Do your learners have a motivation or intention that provides them with a focus?
- What do they concentrate on as they engage in their work?
- What prior knowledge are they drawing upon? What connections are they creating?
- How does the feedback provided inform their thinking?
- To what extent does the instructional routine allow for this process of reflection and engagement to happen?

In the past two decades, there have been considerable strides in our knowledge about the brain and its application to the world of education with regard to how we handle chronic stress, the manner in which the brain rewires itself, how nutrition impacts cognitive health, and the extent to which our physical environments shape the learning experience (Jensen, 2008). Not only does such research shed light on what makes a particular curriculum design or instructional strategy effective, but it also provides us with better stories to share with our students about what learning is supposed to feel like. Below are seven seminal statements that, if acted upon in the classroom, would significantly increase the amount of learning that would occur. These statements are not intended to be exhaustive in scope or in explanation, but rather to serve as a way to spark your individual and collective exploration of the science of learning.

1. New knowledge is built as an extension of existing knowledge. In order for students to be successful, they must be able to think of what they are being asked to do and consider the task in light of what they have already experienced (Bransford, Brown, & Cocking, 2000).

2. People search their memory banks to retrieve an answer for a given problem or question, and if there isn't one, they must develop a novel solution path. Oftentimes, they will rely on what they already know instead of considering alternate approaches. Instead, tests and assignments in school should not be a function of simple retrieval of information, but rather a more robust measure of students' ability to think critically and communicate their ideas.

3. Novice learners need to acquire factual knowledge in tandem with conceptual understanding in order to be able to think effectively. While many educators have believed for years that students needed to learn "the basics" before they could engage in more higher-order thinking, research reveals that this is not the case (Bransford, Brown, & Cocking, 2000; Willingham, 2009). They must engage in "parallel play"—strengthening their foundation through the application of basics in complex, real-world situations.

4. There are limits on working memory that affect how much information the brain can handle at one time. The design of a task, then, can have a real impact on the likelihood that learners will be able to successfully complete it. Students benefit from an organizational structure including well-defined tasks and clearly stated goals (Willingham, 2009).

5. The quality of focus during learning affects the likelihood of whether something will be remembered. A learner who works quickly to finish an assignment or who is attempting to do multiple tasks simultaneously is less likely to generate rich thinking or discern connections.

6. The motivation and capacity to learn are naturally intrinsic. When a learner is invested in the task, the energy and spirit to do well come from within. We must ensure that students' natural passion to learn is an integral part of our planning.

7. What a learner believes is possible for himself or herself shapes the range of possibilities. The stories that learners conjure up about themselves do matter, and the quality of their thinking affects the quality of the experience. On a regular basis, educators should encourage students to consider the possibilities (both short term and long term) and how to achieve them (Dweck, 2006).

Some of these research findings may be familiar ground to you, either because of personal experience or professional expertise. Other research findings may reinforce or clarify your existing practice. Still other research findings may be surprising because they challenge the limits on what you have already decided is possible for you and for other learners. While this section is by no means an exhaustive discussion of the science of learning, its purpose was to inspire those who design and participate in learning experiences to understand the nature of learning more deeply.

Moving to Action: The Need to Establish Learning Principles

What Can One School or School System Do?

The articulation of learning principles can guide the design of curriculum, assessment, and instruction in a learning organization. By transforming research findings into a set of learning principles—what we currently know to be true about learning—we have the opportunity to improve instructional practices within and across classrooms. Grant

Wiggins and Jay McTighe (2007) offer 10 learning principles based on their own research, analysis, and experience:

1. The goal of all learning is fluent and flexible transfer—powerful use of knowledge, in a variety of contexts.

2. Meaning is essential to learning, hence it is essential to teaching and assessing: learning goals must make sense to the teacher and to the learner. There must be regular opportunities to see the value of what we are asked to learn, how it relates to past learning and how it will relate to future learning.

3. Successful learning requires metacognition: learning how to reflect, self-assess, and use feedback to self-adjust. These metacognitive processes can (and should) be taught explicitly.

4. The complexity of learning requires teachers to draw upon a rich repertoire of teaching and assessing strategies carefully matched to the learning goals.

5. Learning is most effective when differences in learners' prior knowledge, interests, and strengths are accommodated.

6. Greater learning depends upon the right blend of challenge and comfort—knowing that success is attainable, and realizing that persistent effort will pay off.

7. To maximize learning, learners need multiple opportunities to practice in risk-free environments, to receive regular and specific feedback related to progress against standards, and timely opportunities to use the feedback to redo and improve.

8. All learning-related work in schools should be judged against standards related to learning goals (for both students and adults) and reflecting how people learn.

9. As a model learning community, a school appropriately requires learning from every member of its community, since continual learning is vital for institutional as well as personal success.

10. All learners are capable of excellent work, if the right conditions for learning are established. (pp. 113–114)

Once articulated and established in a school, learning principles function like an education "bill of rights": a lens through which all curriculum, instruction, and assessment practices can be viewed to determine whether or not a given practice is in service to the school's mission of understanding. Also, the principles can guide and depersonalize decision making about learning-related issues, such as teaching practices, selection of instructional resource materials, and school policies and structures (e.g., grading and reporting). Whether using an established set of principles (there are many strong collections that have been produced by educational institutions and associations) or starting from scratch, the ownership of these truths is vital to improving the spirit and success of the learner in schools.

Moving to Action: The Need to Establish What Doesn't Work in Schools

What Can One School or School System Do?

Not only is it important to explore and put forth those findings that will best support student learning, it is also important to examine common but misguided strategies to raise student achievement that have backfired. Four such strategies are explored in this section: extrinsic motivation, praising students' intelligence, tolerating student disengagement, and lowering expectations.

Why Extrinsic Motivation Doesn't Work

Faced with increasing demands to get better results and with students who seem reluctant to invest themselves in improving their performance (or uninterested in doing so), many educators have designed reward systems to spur improved achievement. Concern about extrinsic motivation is not new in education literature or staff conversations. I remember a teacher who complained that her superintendent forbade the staff giving students candy as a reward. She wanted to know my "professional opinion" on whether she should do it anyway. Consider what lies beneath the surface of this seemingly straightforward query:

- From the teacher's point of view, should she defy her boss and do what she believes will work for her students?
- From her superintendent's point of view, should staff be permitted to use strategies in the classroom that don't work?

- What about the student's point of view? What effect does candy distribution have on learning?

The short-term excitement caused by reward systems detracts from the present moment. In other words, the prize becomes the point of the activity, which makes deep knowledge and inquiry less likely to occur. Score one for the superintendent? Not exactly. While the decree may have been well-intentioned, the thorny problem still remains that if the work students are expected to do offers minimal opportunity for engagement or flow, why should they care about doing it? What if receiving candy causes them to do something as opposed to nothing? Consider widely popular reading competitions—what if meeting the challenge of reading 1,000 books in a month gets students reading who would otherwise never pick up a book outside of class time? Extrinsic motivation is viewed by many educators as better than no motivation at all. Let's go back to the candy example. If the design of the learning is not intrinsically rewarding, then at least the candy creates some incentive for students to perform. Consider another common scenario: a teacher or principal offering students a pizza party if everyone does well on the next test. Students complete their assignments on time, cheer each other on to do their best, and are elated when they get their prize. But the second reward never produces quite the same result; and by the third time this system is implemented, students want to know what else you have to offer. Sometimes students perform more poorly during a reading challenge program because they become fixated on racing through text instead of deriving meaning from it. Such anecdotes are common when students expect incentives in order to learn.

Not only does this "what's in it for me" mind-set become increasingly expensive, but the use of such extrinsic motivators can actually negatively affect performance, dull thinking, and block creativity. In a July 2009 TED (Technology, Entertainment, Design) Talk, Daniel Pink builds a persuasive case about the limitations: "These contingent motivators—if you do this, then you get that—for a lot of tasks, they either don't work or they do harm. This is one of the most robust findings in social science and also one of the most ignored." Pink goes on to describe how on challenging tasks that require innovative or agile thinking, numerous research studies reveal that the greater the incentive, the worse the performance. While this finding may appear counterintuitive, the reason is that the incentive narrows thinking, because the participant develops tunnel vision in the fixation on completing the task. Complex problems, however, require the implementation of innovative approaches. Those participants unencumbered by a reward more readily considered alternate strategies and generated more powerful results. A 21st century curriculum should be defined by authentic tasks that require students to apply what they have learned to solve unfamiliar problems; develop new solution paths; and create new ideas, products, and texts. These tasks require thinking outside of the box, which means that tunnel vision triggered by external motivators impedes students' success in completing the task.

Why Praising Students' Intelligence Doesn't Work

Research on praise is surprisingly clear: students who are praised for their intelligence become trained to equate success with intelligence and failure with stupidity. Not only does this inhibit students from taking on more challenging problems, but it also flies in the face of the science about learning.

> The problem with praising kids for their innate intelligence is that it misrepresents the neural reality of education. It encourages kids to avoid the most useful learning activities, which is learning from mistakes. Unless you experience the unpleasant symptoms of being wrong, your brain will never revise its models. Before your neurons can succeed, they must repeatedly fail. There are no shortcuts for this painstaking process. (Lehrer, 2009, pp. 53–54)

> After seven experiments with hundreds of children, we had some of the clearest findings I've ever seen: Praising children's intelligence harms their motivation and it harms their performance. How can that be? Don't children love to be praised? Children love praise and they especially move to be praised for their intelligence and talent. It really does give them a boost, a special glow—but only for the moment. The minute they hit a snag, their confidence goes out the window and their motivation hits rock bottom. If success means they're smart, then failure means they're dumb. That's the fixed mindset. (Dweck, 2006, p. 175)

Many teachers (and parents) are quite certain that these research findings cannot be true. They regularly lavish praise on their students to show genuine affection and belief in their potential. But if the brain learns through failure, then students must become accustomed to struggle, uncertainty, and constructive criticism. Therefore, adults should instead build students' self-confidence through praising their effort, persistence, tenacity, and courage.

Why Tolerating Student Disengagement Doesn't Work

Despite genuine concerns that students are going through the motions of school instead of being engaged in meaningful learning experiences, most teachers operate as if this is an unfortunate reality of teaching "today's kids." These are kids who supposedly have no attention span, no desire to listen to authority figures, no desire to interact with people in a physical community (as opposed to a virtual one), no desire to better anyone except themselves, no desire to do the grunt work required in order to improve, no desire to be creative, and no desire to worry about the plight of other people. "These kids" supposedly care more about status—cell phones, latest fashions and video games, favorite celebrities—than substance. They are believed to be content to wander through their lives and expect that it will all just work out for them, that at some point they will figure out what they want to do with their lives. And until then, school is something to be tolerated because the adults said so.

Student disengagement affects more than the energy level in the classroom, it also affects students' development as a workforce. Christensen and colleagues (2008) contend that economic prosperity has an impact on the urgency that students have to excel at school:

> Many no longer need to endure studying subjects that are not fun for them. The same downward trend is now beginning in Singapore and Korea. As their economies have prospered, a smaller portion of their students are studying math and engineering because the extrinsic motivation has disappeared—and there is precious little intrinsic motivation, given the way these subjects are taught. (p. 8)

In other words, those who are determined to use education as a springboard for a better life will endure longer school days, intense study sessions, didactic instruction, and little leisure time. When success in school is clearly connected to a better way of life, the motivation and commitment of students and their families are intense. But when a prosperous future has been achieved, when generations of students are raised already living a comfortable life, motivation levels can decline precipitously. Consider the following description of a homework review routine in a classroom lesson.

The first bell rings and students slowly begin to file into the room. The teacher greets them and tells them what tasks to do once they sit down. Most students dutifully take out their homework from the previous night as well as something to write with. Some students just sit, looking exhausted, lost, or worn out before they've even begun. And then the work begins.

"Take out your homework."

"Take out your homework." (A second time.)

"I'm going to come around and check it while you look at the answers to the problems that I have posted on the board. Your job is to identify the ones that you had difficulty with, and we'll go over them together."

All students look up and down from their paper to the board and back again as they begin to erase and replace any problem-solving evidence that is different from what appears on the board. Some students are copying very quickly to fill in answers to problems that they didn't know how to do, or just didn't attempt.

"What questions do you want to review?"

Silence.

"I know from looking at the assignments around the room that many of you struggled with at least three or four of the problems up there. This is your opportunity to understand better."

Silence.

"I already know how to do all of these problems. This is your last chance. Otherwise we are moving on."

One student raises his hand to ask the teacher a question. She brightens when she sees the hand go up, but loses heart when she hears that the basis of the student question has to do with her handwriting, not the subject matter. After her perfunctory response, silence takes over the classroom again.

"OK, if you don't have any questions, then we will move on. You have to remember, kids, that you are responsible for knowing this stuff. You will be tested on it in a couple of days. I need you to be active in your own learning. You can't expect me to care more than you do."

The kids settle into their seats a little more, as if to get comfortable for the lecture they are about to receive about accountability, responsibility, and the relevance of school to the real world. The lecture is familiar, but has little impact on their performance.

A brilliant mathematician who had embarked on a second career as a high school teacher provided a painful illustration of the extent of this malaise. He taught juniors at an elective magnet school for mathematics and science. For the first several months of the year, his students were in constant agony from the dual challenges of learning rigorous mathematics and a lack of an established procedure to apply to the problems. Instead of being inspired by the opportunity to discover solution paths, students were aggravated that the solutions were so elusive.

The teacher decided to try an experiment: he made the next series of lessons as rote as possible so that he could break his students of their desire to reduce math to a series of procedures in a toolbox. He gave students dozens upon dozens of problems that were virtually identical in nature, requiring little more than the predictable application of a procedure and computational accuracy. The kids began to relax, smiled more, and completed their homework with increased regularity and enthusiasm. One student even asked the teacher if he could keep teaching this way for the rest of the year, because now math made sense to him again. The teacher was devastated by how deeply entrenched students' misunderstandings about the power of mathematics were— they felt a greater sense of accomplishment in doing uninteresting work than they did in struggling to harness the power, beauty, and elegance of mathematical expression. After relating this story to me, the teacher wondered aloud, "Is it too late to teach them mathematics?"

This heartfelt question has been posed by so many teachers in various forms:

- Is it too late for reading to be a pleasurable experience?

- Is it too late for students to become curious about how data are collected and presented and the impact data have on an audience?
- Is it too late for students to become compassionate toward others?
- Is it too late for students to become deliberate about the words they choose to express themselves?
- Is it too late for students to become more interested in the world than in their own self-interests?
- Is it too late for school to become a place that makes students excited about what they're going to learn today?

As discussed in the first part of the chapter, it is never too late to retrain our brains. However, such retraining requires fundamentally different learning experiences so that students grow to value the pursuit of inquiry, the depth of analysis, and the development of ideas.

Why Lowering Our Expectations Doesn't Work

When teachers design learning tasks to be easy out of fear that students won't be able to "get it" if the tasks are challenging and won't care enough to try, they assume more of the responsibility for doing the work. They end up more exhausted, and students end up more passive, further alienated by the lack of challenge in the work. When teachers provide students with study aids, lecture notes, review checks, and practice exams to support their achievement, they overlook the more fundamental issue that inhibits achievement: many students do not understand the work they are doing because their learning keeps them at the surface level of knowledge. Teachers remain the experts—the ones who have conceptual fluency, who have command of factual information, who can recognize patterns, and who can see the deep structure of problems. Many teachers have explained to me that their students are not capable of engaging in this level of work, pointing to the current lack of motivation and low achievement results as evidence. They conclude that they have no choice but to continue to "dumb down" the work so that anyone can do it; they tell me that the job of teachers is to teach the kids they have, not the kids they wish they had in front of them. They operate according to an unexamined assumption that if the work is easy enough, students will build up their self-confidence, feel good about school, and begin to engage in more rigorous work. Parker J. Palmer (1998) suggests that educators examine the assumptions we have made about the capabilities of our students:

> The way we diagnose our students' condition will determine the kind of remedy we offer. . . . The dominant diagnosis, to put it bluntly, is that our "patients" are brain-dead. Small wonder, then, that the dominant treatment is to drip data bits into our students' veins, wheeling their comatose forms from one information source to the next until the prescribed course of treatment is complete, hoping they will absorb enough intellectual nutrients to maintain their vital signs until they graduate. . . . But the power of this self-fulfilling prophecy seems to elude us: we rarely consider that our students may die in the classroom because we use methods that assume they are dead. (p. 42)

The challenge for educators is to develop innovative ways to engage students in the exploration of conceptual threads and develop fluency with key rules and skills that define the discipline. By changing our assumptions and trusting students as learning partners, teachers shift their focus away from giving students information and toward equipping students to think deeply and flexibly about their subject.

Unfortunately, even the research about how people learn and the vision of what students can do are not sufficient for some of my readers, who remain stuck because of what they experience on a daily basis. They subscribe to two beliefs:

- It's not possible here.
- Even if it were possible, I don't know how to make it happen. I don't know what it would look like.

Let go of your certainty of what can't happen for a little while as you consider the following reflection question.

Reflection Question

What if my students found joy and purpose in their work?

Wanting Something More for Our Students

When you show up to learn, you bring your heart, your tenacity, your passion. You bring your prior experiences and leverage them any way you know how to try to make today's challenge successful. And when you fail, whether in dramatic fashion or in quiet confusion, you are determined to figure out what went wrong so that next time will be better. You are resolute in wanting to achieve better results and relentless in seeking out additional resources to make that happen. And when you succeed, it is truly an accomplishment. You find satisfaction not only with where you have arrived but also in the rigor of the process. It means something. You create solution paths that previously were invisible to you, you give form to an idea through the creation of images and the crafting of language, you give voice to a point of view, and you give curiosity an avenue to be explored. You cultivated an original thought, you mastered a significant skill, and you honed a seminal task.

There is a visible difference between engagement and compliance in the classroom—the distinction between those students intrinsically motivated to "get it" and those who do as they're told. A high school student wrote to me about this distinction based on an article of mine he read in class:

> With the way you categorized learners I think I am a compliant learner. I think that because most of the time I try to find the simple answer to the complex question. I also almost never think deep enough to try to prove a point or get a new or different idea. But I can notice the people who are the engaged learners. They are the people who usually get the better grades. But they are also the people who get into the arguments and the class discussions and bring up good points. I noticed that engaged learners are also the ones who have more fun and don't get bored.

This student acknowledges that the experience of other students in the class is not the same as his own, but does not offer any commentary as to why. How painful it must be for students to endure a minimum of six hours per day in a learning environment that does not inspire them (and how painful it must be to teach them). Students are not the only ones able to differentiate between engaged students and compliant students; so, too, can their teachers. With no advanced reading or prior conversation about the subject, staff at the Burnaby School District in

British Columbia, Canada, quickly established consensus about the distinctions between compliant and engaged learners; their conclusions are shown in Figure 5.1.

As the staff members were close to finishing the task, several of them began to openly wonder about the emergence of an unsettling idea: compliant students are easier to teach. After a little more reflection, they modified the idea, realizing that compliant students are actually harder to teach, but easier to manage. Engaged learners can display annoying behaviors, such as being so immersed in something that they ignore directions, being preoccupied with something that is not in the scope of the expected performance, or turning work in late because it just wasn't ready to be finished yet.

In another of my workshops, a group of library media specialists in western New York were given a similar task: describe the difference between a compliant researcher and an inquisitive researcher. They were asked not only to describe the differences but also to make the language of the descriptors visual enough that their work could be used as the basis for a classroom observation tool. After 30 minutes of brainstorming and 60 minutes of revision, they produced the table in Figure 5.2.

After the table was completed, I asked workshop participants, "How would you rate the students in your library right now?" All of them quickly agreed that the compliant learners vastly outnumbered the inquisitive ones. I followed up by asking, "So, how does the way you (library media specialist, classroom teacher, and students) work favor compliance over inquisitiveness?" The key points they raised included the following:

• Insufficient time to complete research tasks means that students are racing to find sources as quickly as possible, regardless of their validity or relevance.

Figure 5.1	Distinctions Between Compliant Learners and Engaged Learners	
	Compliant Learners	Engaged Learners
Emotion	• Have flat energy • Show little, if any emotion	• Experience an emotional rollercoaster • Are willing to be angry and frustrated • "Wow, that's cool!" • Are emotionally charged—impulsive, passionate, frustrated
Perseverance	• Easily meet deadlines • Like to be finished • Are reluctant to revise • Like to get tasks off the "to do" list • See success as the end point	• Invest themselves in the work • Want to persevere • Care about the details • Want to get it right • Are willing to keep going • See success as the starting point for the next question/outcome
Questioning	• What do I do? • Does this count? • How much do I have to do? • Listen	• What if . . . ? • How about this? • Questions connect to previous learning • Inquiry-based • Thinking • Focused, penetrating
Creativity	• Wait for someone to come up with an idea • Look around to see what others are doing • Ask teacher for guidance • Feel contained • Receive information	• Collaborate • Draw, build • Are open to a variety of solutions • Feel free and resilient • Process and apply information "off point"
Pathways	• Want teacher to choose • Prefer a familiar path	• Create their own pathways, often multiple ones • Embrace the new/challenging
Behavior	• Obedient • Predictable • Well-behaved • On task	• Unpredictable • Disruptive • Critical • Ask challenging questions • Impulsive with interesting ideas • Can be frustrating for adults

Source: Burnaby Schools, British Columbia, Canada. Reprinted by permission.

Figure 5.2	Compliant Researchers Versus Inquisitive Researchers
A Compliant, Dutiful Researcher . . .	**An Inquisitive, Dynamic Researcher . . .**
• Follows oral and/or written directions with minimal prompting. • Completes explicit procedures and requirements in a timely manner. • Focuses on task completion, not communication with others. • Independently searches for answers to straightforward questions and seeks assistance for searches involving complex questions. • Seeks approval, credit, and/or high marks because of the amount of research found (not synthesis or knowledge construction). • Seeks approval, credit, and/or high marks because of the attention to visual details (not substance of message, content, or connections). • Elects to follow known procedures, explore familiar topics, utilize tools that he or she already has fluency with, and dismisses alternative points of view or approaches. • Asks for direct instruction from staff to complete tasks and/or navigate tools he or she has already been taught multiple times. • Conducts research with no expectation for personal relevance, connection, or interest. • Dismisses information and/or points of view that don't fit with research collected so far. • Records information regardless of credibility of source or relevance to topic or task.	• Focuses on pursuit of the inquiry and/or deepening understanding of the content, sometimes in lieu of completing task requirements and finishing in a timely manner. • Moves quickly from one location (physical zone, Web site, book) to another because of the fast-paced nature of his or her thinking and what he or she wants to explore next. • Expands the boundaries of the inquiry based on what is personally interesting and relevant. • Pursues own train of thought regardless of task at hand or feedback from staff. • Strives to fully understand an issue, topic, or problem through the exploration of the accepted/popular point of view as well as alternate/divergent points of view. • Relies on personal preferences and/or tools to record and synthesize information. • Constructs knowledge through the creation of connections and deliberate use of evidence within and across sources. • Seeks assistance from staff after exhausting all known strategies for finding information sources and/or investigating credibility. • Shares interesting information, concepts, and sources with others without prompting or consideration for those around him or her. • Demands immediate assistance, attention, and/or conversation based on his or her deep connection to the research.

Source: School Library System, Onondaga-Cortland-Madison BOCES, Syracuse, New York. Reprinted by permission.

• Insufficient development of information literacy and technology skills means that students have limited strategies to locate appropriate information.

• Research task only requires information acquisition and summarization—there is no meaningful opportunity for students to pose and pursue a research question, analyze information, and synthesize findings.

• Students prefer finding sources to reading them, want to find direct answers to direct questions, and don't enjoy struggle.

• Students who are inquisitive and dynamic are difficult to work with—they can be impulsive, stubborn, animated, and/or lost in their own train of thought.

After discussing these points, one participant shared this insight: "We [library media specialists] are so busy running the library that compliant learners have become 'good enough' for us. In fact, sometimes they represent the on-task kids, the kids we ask other kids to emulate." Think about that statement for a while. Wouldn't you rather have a class full of engaged learners who demonstrate the tenacity, commitment, and passion to explore the unknown, ruminate over an "impossible" task, and reconsider known knowledge?

In Pursuit of Purpose

In addition to engagement in the present moment, learners should feel greater connection between their schoolwork and their life's work. While some educators believe that children are too young to know what they want to do when they grow up, the power to articulate a goal and then go after it—the development of purpose—has a significant impact on a child's motivation, focus, resilience, and success. The search for such a goal, however, begins with an exploration of personal interests, talents, and ambitions. In the book *Path to Purpose*, William Damon (2008) encourages educators to counsel students in a way that enables them to pursue their own purpose:

Young people treasure guidance from experienced adults who care about them and know more about the world than they do. To be most helpful—and welcome—the guidance must speak to the youngster's highest aspirations. But it does not need to humor unrealistically romantic dreams about mastering the universe. Young people do not wish to be shielded from hard realities; they wish to learn how to accomplish their dreams in the face of such realities. Informing them of the actual steps they must take in order to achieve their highest aspirations is educative in the best sense of the word. (p. 124)

Reflection Question

What do our students want to be when they grow up? How might their responses impact their motivation to learn? How might their responses impact the way we teach?

At what age should we begin to ask our students what their purpose is? Most commonly, we ask it of our youngest students, albeit usually superficially. Students in the primary grades often dream big about what they want to do when they become adults. At these young ages, many students imagine assuming the career mantle of one of their parents or of one of their personal heroes (real or imaginary). My 3rd grader has narrowed it down this week to being a chef, teacher, librarian, or world traveler. The point of asking the question is to encourage them to dream big about all that is possible and to begin to discover what makes them special—their unique talents, strengths, and capacities. Damon (2008) recommends that educators close the "meaning gap" between what students do in school and what students hope to accomplish as a result of their education:

> In our secondary schools and colleges alike, few instructors spend time discussing with students the wider meaning of what they are doing day to day—an odd omission for institutions dedicated to intellectual examination and critical questioning. This "meaning gap" extends from the student's present activities to his or her future prospects: in both cases, students too often are mystified about the relevance of their school work to the knowledge skills they will need to use. In a broader sense, it is even less likely that classroom instruction will lead students to reflect on such essential questions as "what kind of person do I want to become?" or

"what is the meaning of my life?" Such questions seem too airy for many educators, even in philosophy courses. Yet they are central to becoming a fully educated person. (pp. 114–115)

Damon takes the original question "What do you want to be when you grow up?" to another level of depth, asking "What do you want to contribute to the world?" After surveying several thousand students on these two questions, it becomes clear that their responses center much more on career aspirations than on global contributions, and that the reasons behind their aspirations are often missing or vague. In one school district, we surveyed students on their goals and got the following responses:

- Female, 7th grader: "I would like to be an author when I get older. I enjoy writing fictional stories because I can get lost into my own little world and it's enjoyable."
- Male, 8th grader: "I want to be an inventor because I like inventing stuff to make everyday life easier."
- Female, 9th grader: "I want to be a zoologist and write for *National Geographic* magazine. I love working with animals, science, and I love to travel/write. It would be the perfect occupation for all the things I love."
- Male, 11th grader: "Social action lawyer. It combines two elements I really enjoy, debate and social/community advocate."
- Female, 12th grader: "I want to work in theater as an actress and as a screenwriter; I love being on stage and it's my best way of expressing myself."

While every student surveyed offered at least one answer about future aspirations, two key questions arise based on their responses. First, how clear are students on what these aspirations entail? Second, how clear are staff on what students' aspirations are and how they can be used to make the design of school more powerful and relevant? In answer to the first question, many students can readily name a vocation, but they often have little information about what their career choice requires or the likelihood of personal success. Damon suggests that students' responses often are superficial:

> The root of the problem is that, while thinking about their future work, they consider only surface features of the vocation: what's in it for them, whether or not the work seems like it will capture their interest, the possibilities of fame and fortune, without considering what they are trying to accomplish and how their own particular aptitudes could be of use to the world beyond the self. (Damon, 2008, p. 47)

Children's lack of clarity, however, is perpetuated by a dearth of meaningful dialogue from the adults in their lives about what they do for a living and the extent to which their work reflects their own life's purpose. How often do adults discuss what contributions they are making to others through their work? How often do adults describe what it is they do every day? How often do adults describe what it took in order for them to be in their current vocation? How often do adults describe their original aspirations and their future aspirations? These conversations are more necessary than ever before, as what "work" entails in the 21st century can be more difficult to explain:

> Today's workers more often spend their time talking on the phone or clicking on a computer than making tangible goods that a child can appreciate. The child is left with the impression that the only thing that is valuable about the parent's work is the paycheck he or she brings home. (Damon, 2008)

The second question relates to the extent to which staff develop students' path to purpose through the design of curriculum, assessment, and instructional experiences. In high school years, when the question of purpose should begin to loom larger in the minds of students, educators, and parents alike, many students are left to wonder about career aspirations on their own. There often is little space in the four years of high school for students to elect to take courses that correlate with their interests. There is even less clarity about what those courses should even be, based on the career that students intend to pursue. For example, a student interested in running a small business would need a broad range of courses based on the nature of the business (catering, shoe store, convenience store); financial planning to secure a bank loan, pay taxes, and meet payroll; leadership skills to manage and inspire employees; organizational skills to meet key deadlines and expectations;

and the vision to make the business viable (mission statement, location, branding). The tasks we craft for students to accomplish should align with their search to identify goals, priorities, role models, mentors, and heroes for themselves.

Moving to Action

The following actions are intended to open up a multitude of possibilities. The key point, however, is that much can be done with preexisting resources, personnel, and subject area curricula to provide students with more powerful opportunities to discover who they are, what they dream of doing, and how they can create the foundation for that path now.

What Can One Teacher Do?

• Ask students to communicate their aspirations on a sign and hang the class's aspirations on the ceiling.

• Make explicit connections between current learning goals (of the lesson, task, course, or grade level) and student aspirations.

• Tailor learning experiences to provide opportunities for students to explore areas of stated passion, talent, and interest.

• Talk to students about your own goals—what motivated you to become a teacher, how you accomplished that task, and what experiences have proven to be the most satisfying.

What Can One Department or Program Do?

• Design experiences that enable students to communicate and collaborate with peers and mentors within and outside of school to discuss important issues, ask questions and seek information, and seek feedback and support on projects.

• Identify "greats" or "geniuses" in the field (both past and present) so that students can examine the mind-set they adopted, the obstacles they encountered, and the accomplishments or experiences that were most rewarding to those individuals.

What Can One School Do?

• Reexamine the access staff have to students outside of the classroom—library media specialists, guidance counselors, administrators, and others—to create more opportunities for students to seek support and mentorship not because of a crisis situation (as is most common) but because of a shared passion, area of expertise, or personal connection.

• Develop an "advisory period" or mentor system to pair small groups of students with a staff member for the tenure of their time in the building. This type of structure exists in many secondary schools, but may not be as effective as it could be in strengthening relationships or providing guidance to students.

• Engage students in the articulation and development of personal aspirations and concrete actions that they can pursue immediately to work toward those goals.

• Use the interview questions offered by William Damon above to open up the thinking of the student and staff about the motivation for and realization of their aspirations.

What Can One System Do?

• Establish a service project requirement to provide every student with the avenue and opportunity to contribute to the lives of others as they manage a long-term, independently selected project.

• Embed research tasks into various subject-area curricula to train students to explore big questions that they wonder about, complex problems that they want to understand more deeply, and people's lives that they find personally fascinating.

• Create and sustain a robust career center that provides learners with access to job descriptions, standard prerequisites, and training programs for vocations or fields that they are interested in pursuing (both in the short term and in their postsecondary plans).

Conclusion

As Chapter 5 comes to a close, the conversation is about to come full circle: Chapter 6 revisits the myths of Chapter 1 in light of a fresh set of thoughts, possibilities, and expectations. Consider what a learning organization can be for learners and what actions you think are worth pursuing whether in your own classroom, team, department, building, or system. When your thinking changes, your experience changes—not just for you, but also for everyone around you.

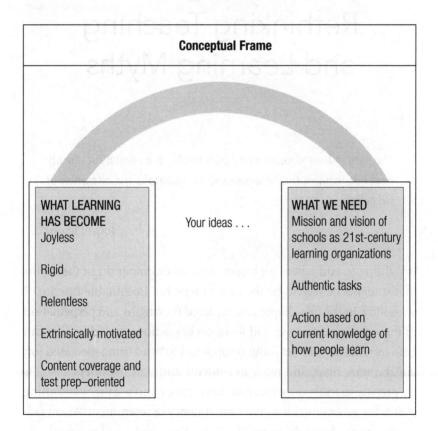

Conceptual Frame

WHAT LEARNING HAS BECOME	Your ideas . . .	WHAT WE NEED
Joyless		Mission and vision of schools as 21st-century learning organizations
Rigid		
Relentless		Authentic tasks
Extrinsically motivated		Action based on current knowledge of how people learn
Content coverage and test prep–oriented		

6

Revisiting and Rethinking Teaching and Learning Myths

The path of least resistance and least trouble is a mental rut already made. It requires troublesome work to undertake the alteration of old beliefs.

John Dewey

It is fitting to end where we began, with an examination of the myths that students believe to be the unfortunate but immutable essence of schooling. In the first chapter, we explored the origins and perpetuation of these realities; now we will focus on key actions and ideas that can help us reframe what learning is supposed to be to bring increased joy, engagement, rigor, and pride to students and staff members alike. As we prepare to focus once more on the myths, try to see them as starting points for generating ideas, not despondency or resentment. After reading this book, the myths should feel less entrenched—and as your thinking changes, so too will the thinking of those around you. This journey to open up space for fresh thought and innovative ideas will be driven by our steadfast determination to live up to our promise. Alongside each of the original myths, I have proposed a new one characteristic of a 21st century learning organization. These new myths are intended to trigger your own ideas in service to your own mission statement. I encourage you to view what's to come as a model of a design exercise that you can replicate in your own schools.

Supplanting the Old Myths

The mission of a 21st century learning organization is to engage all learners in the acquisition of key knowledge and skills and the development of connections so that they can pursue powerful questions, tackle complex problems, collaborate with diverse people, imagine new possibilities, and communicate their ideas.

Myth #1

Replace

> The rules of this classroom and subject area are determined by each teacher.

with

> The rules of this classroom and subject area are defined by the powerful questions and complex problems faced by professionals in this field, citizens who care for their community, and individuals trying to realize their dreams.

The challenge of this myth lies in reframing the role of teacher creativity and innovation in the design of student learning. Students need overwhelming evidence that they can trust that what they are asked to learn today is part of an elaborate, coordinated plan intentionally crafted by staff. As they move from grade level to grade level and building to building, the staff members in front of them will change, but the larger schema will remain the same. This trust is not easily won, especially from students who have experienced the former reality throughout their schooling. Two powerful strategies that create this desired curricular consistency and transparency are to develop macro-level essential questions to define long-standing inquiries, and to develop continua that define how student work is expected to improve over time.

Essential questions at both grade level and building level serve as the foundational inquiries of a subject area. Using these questions to guide students' learning throughout their schooling provides students with a sense of reliability and security that fosters engagement. Figure 6.1 includes a set of essential questions created by grade-level teachers and reading specialists in a K–5 school.

Figure 6.1	K–5 Essential Questions for Reading

KINDERGARTEN	GRADE 1
• What do good readers do? • What do good listeners do? • How do I choose a "just right" book? • What do I think and feel about what I read? Why do I think and feel this way? • What do I notice about the text? How does that affect the way I read? • What's happening in the story? • What do I do when I get stuck? • How do I know if I understand what I'm reading? • What makes me want to read?	• What do good readers do? • What do good listeners do? • How do I choose a "just right" book? • What do I think and feel about what I read? Why do I think and feel this way? • What are my strategies for reading this text? How do I know if they're working? • What do I notice about the text? How does that affect the way I read? • What's happening in the story? • What is the author trying to tell me? • What do I do when I get stuck? • How do I know if I understand what I'm reading? • What makes me want to read?

GRADE 2	GRADES 3–5
• What do good readers do to understand? • What do good listeners do to understand? • How do I choose a "just right" book? • What do I think and feel about what I read? Why do I think and feel this way? • What are my strategies for reading this text? How do I know if they're working? • What do I notice about the text? How does that affect the way I read? • What's happening in the story? • What is the author trying to tell me? How do I support my thinking? • What do I do when I get stuck? • How do I know if I understand what I'm reading? What do I do with that information? • What is the purpose for reading this text? • What makes me motivated to read?	• What habits and routines do lifelong readers develop? • What do I think and feel about what I read? Why do I think and feel this way? • What are my strategies for reading this text? How do I know if they're working? • What kind of text is this? What structures can I expect to see? How does that affect the way I read? • What is the author trying to tell me? How do I support my thinking? • What do I do when I get stuck? • How do I know if I understand what I'm reading? What do I do with that information? • What is the purpose for reading this text? • How does the author make the text come alive?

Source: Mount Pleasant Central School District, New York. Reprinted by permission.

Creating school-based or system-based rubrics to establish levels of quality for a given task emphasizes the direct relationship between what we say we value and what we grade. Students and parents alike believe that what gets measured is what matters; the more consistent the "measuring stick," the more students can apply previous learning experiences to improve their future performance. There are a number of quality scoring tools available online. For those of you who would rather create your own, remember that it is an arduous task that requires a heavyweight team of individuals to ensure that the language is comprehensible, the progression from score point to score point clarifies growth, and the tool will be applicable to a range of tasks (and possibly a range of disciplines).

The consensus-driven development and transparent communication of essential questions and rubrics not only assures students that the work they do today will contribute to their larger education in the subject, but also strengthens the collective curricular, assessment, and instructional practices within the school. There are myriad other consensus-driven practices worth pursuing (e.g., backward-design–based curriculum templates, literature circles, protocols for lab reports, formal exhibitions of creative work). The best ones to pursue are those that are in direct service to your mission statement. Just remember that when you work to improve internal consistency, you should establish how that effort will improve the effectiveness of learning for all students based on research and learning principles. In addition, it is important to clarify where staff remain free to do their own thing in service of the shared learning goals.

Myth #2

Replace

> What the teacher wants me to say is more important than what I want to say.

with

> The purpose of classroom dialogue is to facilitate my construction of knowledge and continued curiosity.

At the heart of this myth is the importance of the learner's voice in the classroom. Therefore, it is vital to openly discuss with your students the extent to which this generalization relates to their own experience in school. This may be a tricky conversation to host face to face, because if students hold the former belief, it is unlikely that they will speak candidly about how they feel. Consider more informal and anonymous ways for students to share their thoughts, such as a student survey, a blog, or a conversation facilitated by someone who is not on the staff. Another approach would be to share with them the following poem and ask them to post their responses on a website or share during a class discussion.

The Student's Prayer, by Umberto Maturana Romesin

> Don't impose on me what you know,
> I want to explore the unknown
> and be the source of my own discoveries.
> Let the known be my liberation, not my slavery.
> The world of your truth can be my limitation;
> your wisdom my negation.
> Don't instruct me; let's walk together.
> Let my riches begin where yours end.
> Show me so that I can stand
> on your shoulders.
> Reveal yourself so that I can be
> something different.
> You believe that every human being
> can love and create.
> I understand, then, your fear
> when I ask you to live according to your wisdom.
> You will not know who I am by listening to yourself.
> Don't instruct me; let me be.
> Your failure is that I be identical to you.

(Poem reprinted by permission of the author.)

An interesting extension of this task would be to have students identify or create an alternate poem that captures their own perspective about the extent to which student ideas are heard in the classroom.

While starting a dialogue is a valuable first step, there must be a more fundamental shift in the design of assessment and instructional practices. If we want our learners to believe that their voices, thinking, and conceptions matter, we must create opportunities for them to pursue those ideas as part of their schoolwork. The most natural way to do this is by consistently differentiating learning experiences at the classroom level. Teachers can collaborate with their students to tailor individual assignments so that the content, process, and product maximize interest while also demonstrating evidence of learning goals. Some examples of differentiation follow:

• Students can work on the reading comprehension skill of main idea and supporting detail by reading and analyzing a nonfiction text on a topic of high interest to them. They can then report out their information to a small group of their peers (who likely read a different topic) to get feedback from them on their organization of the information as well as whether the report made other students more interested in the topic as well.

• Students can work on finding a viable solution path to a complex math problem over a period of days, if not weeks. The teacher distributes a problem (or several problems) to the class and asks them to work on it until they believe they have a viable solution. They are encouraged to use their peers as sounding boards throughout the process, but are also welcome to work on their own. The final product is the explanation of their reasoning as well as their solution.

• Students can study the same historical event through the lens of different figures to better understand how who you are (what you believe, what you have experienced, etc.) affects your interpretation of what happened, your perception of justice or injustice, and your determination of appropriate actions to take.

• Students can develop a business plan for a company that they would want to run one day so that they can learn about the areas of growth in a local economy, the process of applying for financing, and the process of assembling a network of individuals and businesses to help them bring their concept to market.

Readers may look at these three examples and be underwhelmed; they may believe that this type of work is already happening at the classroom level (and perhaps it is taking place in your classroom!). I would agree that in almost every school I visit, I see pockets of this type of practice. To counteract the myth, however, requires such exemplary practice to become the rule, not the exception to the rule.

Educators must consistently invite students to offer their ideas for how to make their work more meaningful—which likely will engender more rigor, responsibility, and ownership of the work in students. The more connected students are to their work, the more likely they are to enjoy the experience (think back to Chapter 4). Conversely, the more they are merely going through the motions—the more they are repeating what the teacher or the text said—the less likely the learning experience will have the intended long-term effect. This is the "bad karaoke" described in Chapter 1 that we are trying to break free from; learners should be able to improve their skills and expand their knowledge without having to conform to what the "experts" have decided is true.

Myth #3

Replace

> The point of an assignment is to get it done so that it's off the to-do list.

with

> The most powerful problems are the ones with no obvious solution paths; they help me learn more deeply about the subject and myself.

The most important action to take to counteract the original myth is to make sure that the curriculum gives students and teachers the time to slow down so that they can focus. If curricular topics and skills go flying by in isolation, teachers and students alike scramble to keep up with the pace of activities instead of making meaning from them. The more discrete assignments there are, the less likely that any of those assignments matter. If the curriculum is overloaded with expectations, assignments, and resources that are impossible to accomplish in the allotted time, students do not have the space to learn deeply, and grades are more about a student's ability to consistently manage the work than achievement in a particular subject.

Classroom teachers and curriculum leaders must collaborate to produce a guaranteed and viable curriculum. Even though it has a significant impact on student achievement (Marzano, 2003), most schools lack such a curriculum. "Guaranteed" means that all students have the opportunity to achieve the learning goals of the unit and course (regardless of teacher or how students are grouped). "Viable" means that it is possible for the desired learning to occur within the given time available. Many curriculum documents are built on the assumption that every school day is available for teaching and learning, which is just not accurate given test preparation, test days, and planned and unplanned interruptions. To make matters worse, every day is often "spoken for" on pacing guides and unit calendars, leaving no space for students to pursue tangents, to get stuck and try again, to spend more time when an interesting idea is shared, to revise their assignments, to conference with their peers or their teacher, or to celebrate their accomplishments.

Take a moment to read the following poem.

Fire, by Judy Sorum Brown

What makes a fire burn

is space between the logs,

a breathing space.

Too much of a good thing,

too many logs

packed in too tight

can douse the flames

almost as surely

as a pail of water would.

So building fires

requires attention

to the spaces in between,

as much as to the wood.

When we are able to build

open spaces

in the same way

we have learned

to pile on the logs,

then we can come to see how

it is fuel, and absence of the fuel

together, that make fire possible.

> We only need to lay a log
> lightly from time to time.
> A fire
> grows
> simply because the space is there,
> with openings
> in which the flame
> that knows just how it wants to burn
> can find its way.

Source: A Leader's Guide to Reflective Practice (p. 12), by Judy Sorum Brown, 2006. © 2003 by Judy Sorum Brown. Reprinted by permission.

Learners need the space to breathe, to think, to reflect, and to reconsider. They need time to think about a question before they answer, and teachers need to give them that time by remaining silent until a student volunteers an idea. It may be a simple premise, but it is often ignored in favor of making every topic and standard a priority. Ultimately, the best way to challenge the original myth is to design curricula that establish clear learning priorities and provide ample time and resources in order for every learner to be successful. Be relentless until this has been achieved, because the quality of your students' thought depends upon it. Learning organizations are not successful when teachers teach; they are successful when students learn.

Another important strategy is to ruthlessly examine every assignment to eliminate "busy work." A group of math teachers I worked with in Texas took this idea to heart and redesigned the way they assign homework. We developed the idea of a "gateway problem"—a problem that students complete during the last 5 to 10 minutes of class. Students are instructed that their performance on the gateway problem influences what problems they will have for homework that night (or whether they will have homework at all). Students were initially skeptical that there would be a correlation between their current performance and their homework assignments; they did not think that homework was based on what they needed, but rather on what the textbook or teacher thought should be done next. Once they became acclimated to the practice, they began to realize that the more focused they were on the gateway problem, the less busy work they had for homework. They had every incentive to reveal what they could do for teachers, even though the gateway problems were not graded. As students complete the problems, the classroom teacher circulates around the room and observes their work to determine what problems on that night's assignment are relevant to each student.

A third strategy to foster students' connection to schoolwork is to design tasks for students that are designed to stick around for a while—keeping them on the to-do list. For example, provide students with a problem situation, community issue, inquiry, or ethical dilemma and ask them to sit with that task for days, if not weeks or months. The intention of introducing a task that lingers is for students to learn how to sit with their thoughts. By going through an incubation period where they are expected to think about the task without actually performing it, they train their minds to create new connections and identify additional areas where they need more information. The intent of these tasks is to have students experience being stuck and being poised for a breakthrough while actively waiting for it.

Myth #4

Replace

> If I make a mistake, my job is only to replace it with the right answer.

with

> Failure is an unavoidable part of learning that requires the courage to persevere and the determination to make sense of the flaws.

The first strategy to challenge this myth is to analyze summative assessments used to evaluate and report student achievement to determine the level of thinking they require.

For tests or examinations, consider the following questions:

• What percentage of assessment items have one right answer (and/or one solution path)? What percentage of items have multiple right answers?

- What percentage of assessment items require recall of what was said or read in class? What percentage of items require analysis and application of knowledge?
- What percentage of assessment items require students to report only their answer? What percentage of items require them to include their thinking?

For projects or performance tasks, consider the following questions as part of your analysis:

- Does the task require students to apply what they have learned to a new problem situation?
- Does the process for completing the task remain authentically messy, or has it been translated into a clean procedure?
- Does the task provide students with the opportunity to pursue individual areas of passion and interest?
- Does the task have a rubric? If so, what does the rubric assign the most value to? How does that impact the authenticity of the task?
- Does the task require students to collaborate? If so, is the collaboration intended to make the work more efficient (by dividing it into parts), or is the collaboration intended to enrich the thinking of the group members?
- Does the task provide students with opportunities to receive substantive feedback and resubmit their work?
- Does the task require research outside of given resources?
- Does the task require students to create a publishable product for a specific audience? If so, do students have the opportunity to find out if the product has relevance or the intended effect for an audience outside of the classroom?

Again, if we want the current situation to change, if we truly value something different, then we have to prove that to the students through the design of the tasks we give them. Remember, what gets measured gets done.

A second strategy to challenge this myth is for mistakes to be viewed by both teacher and student as a more intriguing component of learning. The "erase and replace" mentality does not make anyone in the room smarter. In fact, this approach eliminates the possibility of being curious about the nature of the error in the first place. Students should be expected to analyze their own work to determine the nature of any errors they made and glean what potential learning can come from that. Figure 6.2 depicts a tool developed by teachers to encourage revision as part of a class work or homework routine.

Figure 6.2	Creating and Revising Draft Solutions/Responses	
First Draft	Nature of Error, Misconception, Area of Improvement	Revised Draft, Mindful of Revisions, Adjustments, Improvements
Elementary math example: Identify which fraction is greater by using the > symbol. Explain your answer. 1/4 > 1/3 because 4 is bigger than three and 1 and 1 is the same.	I get confused in fractions that the denominator is different than whole numbers. I need to see what a fraction looks like to get it right so I'm going to draw a picture before I do the problems.	2/3 > 2/8
Middle school writing conference example: Student is doing a good job identifying evidence related to the hypothesis, but the information is planted in the paragraphs, not connected to ideas.	Need to work on using evidence to support thinking instead of just providing it and moving on.	For each piece of evidence, provide a segue from your original point and a sentence following the piece of evidence to reinforce the connection.

Source: Zmuda, A., McTighe, J., Wiggins, G., & Brown, J. (2007). *Schooling by design: An ASCD action tool.* Alexandria, VA: ASCD. © 2007 by ASCD.

This type of error reflection and analysis does require more time to complete, but it also avoids the time-consuming practices of re-teaching material that students never mastered and writing the same comments over and over again on student work without seeing a measurable change in performance over time. Again, in order for mistakes to become a more fruitful opportunity to learn, there must be sufficient space in the curriculum for teachers to explore the students' misconceptions (think back to discussion of Myth #3).

Myth #5

Replace

> I feel proud of myself only if I receive a good grade.

with

> My accomplishments are defined by the goals I struggle to achieve and the rewards that come from that pursuit.

One of the most freeing ideas that I have ever come across is based on the research findings presented in *Mindset*, by psychologist and author Carol Dweck (2006). The premise of her work is that the mind-set people have about their learning affects how they respond to struggle and how that affects their feelings toward learning:

> Growth mindset is based on the belief that your basic qualities are things you can cultivate through your efforts. Although people may differ in every which way—in their initial talents and aptitudes, interests, or temperaments—everyone can change and grow through application and experience. . . . You can see how the belief that cherished qualities can be developed creates a passion for learning. . . . The passion for stretching yourself and sticking to it, even (or especially) when it's not going well is the hallmark of the growth mindset. This is the mindset that allows people to thrive during some of the most challenging times in their lives. (p. 7)

Those learners with a "fixed mindset" have decided that what comes easily is a sign of intelligence, and what is a struggle, or where they fail, is a sign of stupidity. They become comfortable with those subject areas (and with certain tasks within those subject areas) where they have a track record of success. Students with a "growth mind-set," however, believe that they can always improve regardless of whether success comes easily or proves to be more elusive.

Dweck further illustrates this point with studies of junior high school students as they transition into classes with more complex subject material and more rigorous grading practices:

> In our study, only the students with the fixed mindset showed the decline. They showed an immediate drop-off in grades, and slowly but surely did worse and worse over the two years. The students with the growth mindset showed an increase in their grades over the two years. When the two groups had entered junior high, their past records were indistinguishable. . . . With the threat of failure looming, students with a growth mindset instead mobilized their resources for learning. They told us that they, too, sometimes feel overwhelmed, but their response was to dig in and do what it takes. (Dweck, 2006, pp. 57–58)

The struggle to do well affects not only how students feel about their teachers, but also how they feel about the subject area. Their interest in the work declines when their grades do not fit with past patterns of performance. This depression in both performance and attitude can profoundly impact achievement, especially in students who have a tradition of high achievement.

Educators and parents can use this basic distinction between fixed and growth mind-sets to augment hope, resilience, and perseverance in students. Mind-sets are manufactured by the learner based on his or her perception of experience, and therefore can be changed with knowledge about how people learn, strategies to improve performance, and willingness to grow from criticism and failure. Many students marvel at the talent and achievements of pioneers in a particular field without examining the sacrifices, challenges, and effort required to reach such acclaim. By developing a more realistic picture about what it takes to create and sustain success, students become more willing to endure rough patches, revise work until it's right, and develop better support systems with peers and mentors.

In addition to challenging this myth at the cognitive level, it is important to challenge it at the policy level. The conversation about grades and grading policy should remain connected to the larger themes of 21st century schooling and the nature of learning. Key points are summarized below:

• Students need consistent opportunities to fail and then succeed without causing permanent damage to their grades.

- Students need to receive candid feedback on their performance based on established standards of excellence without false praise or biting remarks.
- Students need to revise and/or extend their work instead of letting it go and moving on to the next task.
- Students need to see their achievement as separate from the amount of effort they invested and progress they made.
- Students need to reflect on what they are learning and how they are growing because of the work they have generated as well as their own plans to continue to improve over time.

These points could be incorporated into a schoolwide policy that guarantees students the opportunity to revise their work on summative performance tasks within a defined window of time and the opportunity to turn work in as it is ready, so that they can submit multiple drafts in advance of a deadline to garner more feedback and make needed improvements. The key is to create consistency so that parents and students alike know that grades capture not just a first attempt, but the student's best attempt. For a more in-depth examination of how to reform grading policy, see the work of Ken O'Connor (2009), Tom Guskey (Guskey & Bailey, 2001), and Rick Wormeli (2006) for rich information, strategies, and models for improving the way grades are used to communicate achievement and enhance performance both of individual children and the school.

Myth #6

Replace

> Speed is synonymous with intelligence.

with

> Intelligence is developed through hard work and powerful habits.

This myth is perpetuated by the impossible pace of most curricula, which unfortunately makes those students who learn quickly and who have good recall of information appear to be more intelligent and easier to teach. The strategies discussed under Myth #3 apply here as well—schools should examine every curricular unit, task, and assignment to create more space for students to slow down so that they can truly learn. Students who fly through a series of problems may have calculated the correct answer, but they have no idea what they are actually doing in terms of the scientific laws, the deep structure of the problems, and so on. Students who fly through a text and demonstrate comprehension of it may not be able to identify what makes the use of metaphor powerful or appreciate the craftsmanship of the language. Students who parcel out responsibilities to complete a collaborative task and then reassemble the parts at the end to create a coherent piece may get the work done more efficiently, but they will have had minimal interaction with their teammates and consequently little opportunity to extend their individual or collective thinking. Teachers must ensure that neither they nor their students feel a sense of accomplishment because they finished before the clock ran out. True accomplishment comes from what endures after the learning experience is over.

An interesting twist on this myth, however, is that speed is prized not only by teachers but also by society. Some readers may openly wonder whether it is possible to have students slow down the pace of their thinking, or, for that matter, the pace of their lives (think back to the discussion in Chapter 2 about multitasking and the use of time). You may ask the following questions:

- Is it possible to teach students what they need to know and be able to do and still teach them to think big thoughts?
- Will students be able to handle the frustration of sitting with a question or an assignment with no clear answer, established process, or solution path for extended periods of time?
- What do students have to gain from wondering about larger questions? Isn't that level of abstraction less satisfying than the concrete elements of the discipline?
- With all of the fast-paced technologies that students experience in their daily lives, will they be able to stay focused on a sustained thinking activity?

Other readers may wonder if we have time to deeply engage students given the volume of instructional objectives and mandated assessments. (Think back to the Chapter 4 example of the science teacher who wasn't sure if there was time to "do" science.)

To reconnect the learner to the learning organization requires commensurate commitment and contribution of learners investing themselves in schoolwork. Former mathematics teacher Richard Brady (2008) describes his approach to increasing his students' capacity for "living with questions":

> These students will work hard to find answers, but if they're unable to find them or learn them from someone else, many will let the questions go and move on. Yet living with questions was precisely the approach that enabled Newton and many other great thinkers to come upon their most significant insights. Thus, one of my goals for the year was to ask students to consider questions large enough to require living with, questions that I give them and questions they raise themselves. (pp. 92–93)

In the classroom, we must take our collective foot off the accelerator and transform what is currently a blur of facts, lists, and formulas into a vast panorama of ideas. We must consistently and predictably expect students to do rigorous and inspired work.

Myth #7

Replace

> If I get too far behind, I will never catch up.

with

> The time line for learning is affected by my prior knowledge, intrinsic motivation, and clarity of purpose.

Once students become overwhelmed by the actual or perceived gap between themselves and their peers, they can easily adopt a fixed mindset that they are "stupid" or the subject is "stupid," and they are much more likely to quit trying. Feelings of defeat can render meaningless any positive affirmation, effective instructional strategy, appropriate chunking of curriculum, or remediation model. The real concern is that when students give up (even if they are still going through the motions of doing the work), the gap will only increase, which perpetuates feelings of defeat. The more discouraged students become, the less likely they are to put in the time and energy necessary to improve. Not only does this cycle depress individual student achievement, it also plays a formidable role in the perpetuation of larger achievement gaps. When we look at patterns of underperformance exhibited by groups of students based on gender, race, ethnicity, or language barriers, the problem becomes a self-fulfilling prophecy not just for the students but for the staff as well. "These kids can't . . ." is one of the most dangerous and damaging statements for staff to privately believe or publicly espouse, because it perpetuates the false notion that past performance limits future possibility.

Revisiting the notion of fixed and growth mind-sets is useful here for both teachers and students. A student who is behind must do whatever it takes to catch up, which will require working harder and longer than perhaps anyone else in the class. The role of the classroom teacher and the entire staff is to do whatever it takes to support that child's efforts by removing unnecessary obstacles, creating additional opportunities to learn beyond the standard school day, and tapping into the child's natural strengths as much as possible. Achievement gap literature proves baffling for many, because instead of delineating the instructional strategies that work, authors reiterate that the key is high expectations for every child. One school division, determined to close the achievement gap for black male students, assembled a group of classroom teachers who were getting impressive achievement results from all students in order to better understand what they did that could be replicated. What is fascinating is that the teachers spent much of the time sharing personal experiences of what it felt like to be a student when they were growing up and what it feels like to be one of the few black staff members in their schools. When pressed by school leaders to stop telling stories and to shift their focus to concrete strategies, one teacher quietly stated, "The strategies are the same for all kids. The real difference is whether the kids believe you think it is possible for them. I do not let my children fail." Further dialogue revealed that this was the predominant difference: not letting children fail meant that teachers quietly but relentlessly insisted that when the work wasn't good enough, the student did it until it was.

This approach is grounded in unwavering faith in children's capacity and respect for struggle. Teachers must openly challenge the misconceptions that intelligence is fixed and that hard work is for the weak. Willingham (2009) remarks:

> Americans, like other Westerners, view intelligence as a fixed attribute, like eye color. If you win the genetic lottery, you're smart; but if you lose, you're not. This notion . . . has implications for school and work. One implication is that smart people shouldn't need to work hard to get good grades—after all, they are smart. As a corollary, if you work hard, that mean you're not smart. The destructive cycle is obvious: students want to get good grades so that they look smart, but they can't study to do so because that marks them as dumb. In China, Japan, and other Eastern countries, intelligence is more often viewed as malleable. If students fail at a test or don't understand a concept, it's not that they're stupid—they just haven't worked hard enough yet. This attribution is helpful to students because it tells them that intelligence is under their control. If they are performing poorly there is something they can do about it. (p. 131)

Another example of the commitment to help students work harder comes from a group of English language arts teachers for grades 6–12 who were concerned about the reading achievement of their students. Not only were test scores low, but students verbally and nonverbally communicated their boredom, frustration, and lack of connection to what they were asked to read. (In addition, student behavior was relatively unchanged when students were given the opportunity to select their own texts.) Staff first devoted several hours to collating the following advice for students to offer them solace and guidance when they feel frustrated by their reading ability or experience:

1. Give it time—Give it a chance.

2. Get your bearings—Find a roadmap, relax and read it over, check your perceptions.

3. Define the moment—Know when you are in the zone.

4. Shift happens—Understand that your brain fades in and out.

5. Be aware of distractions—Recognize your distractions and adapt your behavior.

6. Switch it up—Approach reading in different ways, both mental and environmental.

7. What do I want?—Have a goal for reading. What do you want to learn? What do you want to experience?

8. Face your fears—Stop, look, and reframe.

9. Recognize and accept tone—Know how your author "sounds." Let your author have his or her own voice.

10. Describe the problem—Learn to talk to yourself and others about what the problem is.

11. Play ball—Come together with other readers to share perceptions.

12. You don't have to love it—You might have to read it.

Staff then created an "instructional playbook" to create more successful reading experiences for their students under varying conditions. They framed this sentiment in their own words and made it the title of a table, an excerpt from which appears in Figure 6.3.

Figure 6.3	Strategies for Increasing Reading Performance
All students are capable of being powerful readers under the right conditions.	
Tactic	Intent
Visualize what is happening in the text—produce or describe that image	• Strengthen connection to text • Draw on different intelligences
Make connections to real-life situations (e.g., text to self, text to world)	• Strengthen connection to text • Make reading feel more relevant • Evaluate impact of readers' life experience and background on how they interact with the text
Analyze a literary convention or device (setting, characterization, etc.)	• Strengthen deep reading of text • Grow appreciation of craft of writing • Evaluate impact of language on the reader and the reading experience
Ask students what topics, authors, or genres they are interested in before determining book selection	• Increase likelihood that students have a positive experience • Strengthen connection to text

continued

Figure 6.3	Strategies for Increasing Reading Performance (*continued*)
All students are capable of being powerful readers under the right conditions.	
Tactic	**Intent**
Book circles, book talks, book clubs	• Test out connections to text by explaining them aloud to someone else • Listen to connections others are making to reflect on own reading, life experience • Evaluate impact of readers' life experience and background on how they interact with the text
Read a variety of genres	• Expose students to a broader range of reading experiences (text, genre, author, content that they otherwise wouldn't get) • Grow appreciation of craft of writing • Increase likelihood that every reader has a connection to a genre or particular text
Have student select a book independently	• Increase likelihood that students have a positive experience • Strengthen connection to text • Put responsibility, ownership of reading on the shoulders of the student
Enact a program of sustained silent reading	• Strengthen connection to text • Build endurance and focus as readers • Provide opportunity for students to read at natural rate of fluency

Source: South Tama County Community School District, Iowa. Reprinted by permission.

The development of this playbook energized the staff and made them feel an increased sense of efficacy—until someone asked if there would be sufficient time to implement these ideas given "all of the other things on their plate." Once again, we come back to the issue of time. There must be space in the curriculum for students to overcome intellectual, emotional, and interpersonal obstacles without falling behind permanently. There must also be time for the teachers to catch their breath so that they can come up with more responsive and innovative approaches to help every learner be successful. Ironically, much of students' anxiety about being behind originates from the words and actions of their teachers. This truly is one of the most important areas where changing our own thinking and thereby our own experiences can enhance the thinking and experiences of others.

Myth #8

Replace

> The way I want to be seen by my classmates affects the way I conduct myself as a learner.

with

> The way I see myself and the contributions I hope to make affects the way I conduct myself as a learner.

School is a social networking hub for children, and the way they want to be perceived by peers does influence their learning behavior. While teachers cannot change this reality, they can design public and private spaces for students to pursue their individual areas of passion, pose substantive questions, and develop key skills. A more public display of learning necessitates that all students be able to meaningfully engage in the task so that they have something to communicate that not only reveals who they are (or perhaps hope to become) but also meets curricular goals. For example, students can collect examples of indirect expression that they find more powerful, vivid, or beautiful than a direct expression. Whether these phrases are self-generated or published, from an assigned text or a personal selection, or from a novel or song lyrics, students can share a piece of themselves through the way they connect to and interpret text. A second example of a more public display is to put students in teams and give them a real problem to solve—something that is complicated, causing real pain or damage, or compelling because of students' age, cultural frame of reference, or identity. Real problems could include the amount of energy wasted in the school building, safety issues within students' neighborhoods, adults who do not know how to read and feel too embarrassed to learn, pollution in a local lake, the impact of tourists on a local economy, or whether certain texts (print and Web-based) should be banned in schools because of their content or use of language.

More private opportunities to learn are also critical, especially for those students who would otherwise sacrifice their relationship with their teacher for their relationship with their peers. These private spaces become a place for teacher and student to interact away from the potentially judgmental stares of other students. The easiest avenues for private learning are through the use of journals and the quiet modification of assignments to fit the learner's needs.

Journals can be structured as a private narrative or exploration that the student produces to make sense of information and ideas. The role of the teacher is to periodically read the entries to better understand how the student thinks and works (as opposed to evaluating the content of the writing). This is a fragile relationship, in that the teacher is expected to suspend judgment and allow the student's connections, stories, and questions to dominate the space.

Another type of journal is an interactive dialogue between teacher and student—a dynamic correspondence about substantive questions and complex problems that the student continues to explore. This exchange, which can be conducted electronically or on paper, provides a powerful record for student and teacher alike of how ideas develop over time.

Another private learning modification is that students can complete an independent research assignment based on a topic of personal interest either directly or indirectly motivated by the course content. A wonderful example of such an assignment was created by a health education team as part of their district's 11th grade curriculum. Students research a health topic of personal concern to them in order to seek answers to questions that they are already worried about, research sensitive topics in a safe and appropriate manner, verify the credibility of a source and the accuracy of the information, and identify appropriate actions that they can take to protect or improve their health. The demonstration of their research is a private conversation with a health teacher or other appropriate school staff member (such as the guidance counselor, nurse, social worker, or psychologist) about what they have learned as well as a works cited list of what sources they consulted. This approach provides students with the shelter they need to engage in deep research about topics of significance without fear of what their peers would say and without oversimplifying the information into a pamphlet or PowerPoint presentation.

Yet another strategy is the practice of making private modifications to assignments to maximize the rigor and relevance of a task for an individual student without compromising his or her public persona. For example, struggling readers who are embarrassed by reading aloud in front of the class may have a private arrangement with the teacher to practice in advance so they can model fluency and build self-confidence. (Note that this is a very different modification than the removal of responsibility for reading aloud altogether.) These adjustments send a powerful message from the teacher to the student: "I will do whatever it takes to help you succeed." Again, what is critical here is that "whatever it takes" is not the removal of rigor or the lowering of expectations, but rather the achievement of those expectations in a more respectful, responsive learning environment.

Myth #9

Replace

> What I'm learning in school doesn't have much to do with my life, but it isn't supposed to—it's school.

with

> The work I do in school opens up the doors of the real world.

Most of the strategies to challenge this myth were addressed in Chapter 4 in our discussion of the need for authentic tasks. When students are given assignments that mirror the processes and products of professionals, they experience the joy and struggle that come from learning. Ultimately, school provides students with access to the real world, along with the scaffolds and guidance needed to navigate those experiences and grow from them.

There is one additional area that bears mentioning—one critical disconnect between life behind the "schoolhouse gate" and life on the outside: media use. Educators have built many firewalls to block students from being distracted in school in the form of filters on Web sites, bans on certain technology devices, and rules about what networking platforms they are allowed to use, to name a few. Despite some of the misgivings about new technologies felt by older generations (myself included), we cannot teach our students in spite of them; the learning organization must adapt to who students have become in the 21st century—and that means acknowledging the role technologies and media play in students' lives.

Prolific media use provides students with instant access to people, music, images, video, information, games, and opportunities. Rubin (2010) reports that today's youths devote 7 hours, 38 minutes to daily media use, or about 53 hours a week. She continues:

> The numbers zoom even higher if you consider kids' multitasking—such as listening to music while on the computer. Those data show young people are marinating in media for what amounts to 10 hours, 45 minutes a day—an increase of almost 2¼ hours since 2004. (Rubin, 2010, paragraph 6)

Not only does this reveal what students are doing in their spare time, but it also shows that our wonderings about whether students think differently are actually well-founded. According to Marc Prensky (2006),

> Today's game-playing kid enters the first grade able to do and understand so many complex things—from building, to flying, to reasoning—that the curriculum they are given feels to them like their mind is being put in a straitjacket, or that their milk is being laced with sedatives. Every time they go to school they must, in the words of one student, "power down." And it gets worse as the students progress up the grades. Most of today's teachers know little if anything about the digital world of their students—from online gaming, to their means of exchanging, sharing, meeting, evaluating, coordinating, programming, searching, customizing, and socializing. As a result, despite their best efforts, it's often impossible for these adults to design learning in the ways their students need and relish. Laments one frustrated parent, "The cookies on my daughter's computer know more about her interests then her teachers do." (pp. 10–11)

We can—and must—become more responsive to who students are, how they research, how they collaborate, how they navigate texts, how they analyze information, and how they communicate with others. It may be a steep learning curve for some, but there is no other option. Today's students have already blazed their own trails as learners and continue to adapt their behaviors as the technology evolves. We have a lot to learn from one another.

Conclusion

The myths enumerated in our first chapter are not carved in stone. Given enough evidence, students can adopt a more optimistic, empowered, dynamic view of learning. If students believe that they will figure it out, they persevere. If students believe that they are getting stronger, they find even more strength to keep going. If students believe that an idea is worth pursuing, they persevere, regardless of what others say. If students believe that they have a powerful story to tell, they craft it and share it with whoever will listen. If they believe failure is an opportunity, they look at it unflinchingly so that they can learn from it. If students believe that they can solve problems that have stymied the generations before them, they study the past but aren't beholden to it. In a 21st century learning organization, we trust our students as partners in learning, because the quality of their thinking determines the quality of their education.

Author's Note

On March 27, 2010, after handing the manuscript for this book in to the publisher, I had a stroke. In one day, my life forever changed. After my brain surgery, I had to rebuild my language all over again. It is a necessary but difficult act, requiring much perseverance, for a writer to rediscover the words she once knew to be true and breathe life back into them.

Afterword

The way we see leads to what we do; and what we do leads to the results we get in our lives. So if we want to create significant change in the results, we can't just change attitudes and behaviors, methods or techniques; we have to change the basic paradigms out of which they grow.

Stephen Covey

This book was born out of my deep concern that learners have become estranged from school. They arrive at the schoolhouse door full of wonderment, questions, and a desire to explore the world, but the more time they spend with us, the more their natural inquisitiveness slips away. While students receive explicit instructions about what we expect them to do, how we expect them to do it, and when we expect it to be completed, they receive little guidance about what learning is supposed to feel like and how to find the energy to engage in cognitively difficult work. While students are subject to numerous lectures that education is necessary to prepare them for college, for future employment, and for the "real world," college professors, employers, and the general public express serious concerns about whether students receive the preparation they need to be successful. This estrangement not only alienates our students, but also saps the enthusiasm, innovativeness, and resilience of staff. While educators want to improve rigor, relevance, and relationships, they often attempt to do so in addition to their current priorities instead of redefining those priorities. While educators want to see more engagement in and enjoyment of learning, they often enlist strategies and incentives to keep everyone willing to do work that they still find unfulfilling.

This book has followed a deliberate but unpredictable journey to inspire thought about what is possible in our schools, for our students, and for ourselves. Unflinching candor is paired with boundless optimism in my certainty that learning organizations are supposed to be fulfilling, powerful, dynamic places that inspire professional and novice learners alike. It's as if we have been trapped in a jail cell for years, only to realize that the key to the lock is in our own hands.

Reflection Question

If school isn't going well for our learners, ourselves, and our society, how do we begin to imagine a better way?

When confronted with a problem, your brain searches for an answer in its memory banks. If no solution is found there, what do you do next as a learner? Just as important, what do you feel next as a learner? The same two questions are valid even when you search your memory banks and *find* an answer. What do you do next? What do you feel next?

At a workshop I attended, the facilitators instructed us to engage two other people in a conversation about a problem we cared deeply about and had devoted much time to "solving," but still had us stuck. The only rule was that no one was allowed to say anything aloud that they had already thought of before: no familiar anecdotes or analogies, and no repetition of all the reasons why it couldn't be done. It was the most awkward conversation that I have ever engaged in, but one of the most fascinating. Every time I started to open my mouth, I would close it again, self-censoring according to the rule. After a dozen of these false starts, I began to realize that I had become pretty boring to listen to. Let's leave out how I came off to family, friends, and colleagues—I had become boring to myself. I had grown comfortable that any new problem was a familiar problem that I likely had the answer to or some authority to speak on, and become increasingly uninterested in the power of context, perception, and new connections. My brain may be designed to look for a memory-based answer to a question, but it also has the capacity for something more.

While developing the capacity to think deeply and create new connections requires constant practice, the possibility is always there, waiting for you. Simply calling attention to the ability to do so improves the quality of a learning experience. Let's go back to the conversation with the serious problem and the rule that had rendered me mute. I found that when I gave up searching for answers to the problem, I finally started listening to the conversation about it. I became engaged not with the dialogue in my head, but with the thoughts shared by others. As the content and feeling behind their words penetrated, I began to see new connections. And finally, seven minutes into the conversation, I had something to say. It wasn't long, and it wasn't pithy, but it had integrity.

The brain can be trained in how it responds to life. When thought settles down and an individual experiences a reprieve from operating in hyperdrive, insights are possible. Some individuals experience this reprieve through running, others through knitting, others through watching tides ebb and flow, but it is possible for anyone to create space that allows for creativity, wisdom, and insight to show up. Parker Palmer (1993) reminds us about the importance of and responsibility for creating that space:

> So often, I speak to solve problems for people, to give them definitive answers to their questions. Frequently I rush to respond in order to prove my authority or to relieve a moment of classroom tension. I forget that tension can be creative; I fail to give it a chance to draw us into the learning space. I do not allow my students' problems and questions to deepen within them, to do their own educative work. I forget that genuine solutions and authentic answers can only come from within my students, that to "educate" them I must speak words that draw out their understanding rather than impose my own. Even the facts and theories I must speak will not be absorbed if they are not spoken into the receptiveness of a compelling question. (pp. 81–82)

As you continue your journey from here, reevaluate what it is that you know for sure, and what truly is open for reconsideration. While in many ways I have been transformed by my research and work with schools, there is still one area of certainty that remains stronger than ever. *We are born natural learners and, given the right conditions, can always return to that state. We are never too old, too jaded, too broken, or too tired; we just need to step into the space of endless possibilities once again.*

Bibliography

Armstrong, T. (1998). *Awakening genius in the classroom.* Alexandria, VA: ASCD.

Berkun, S. (2008, March 12). Thoughts on Google's 20% time [Online article]. Retrieved July 12, 2010, from http://www.scottberkun.com/blog/2008/thoughts-on-googles-20-time

Brady, R. (2008, Summer). Realizing true education with mindfulness. *Human Architecture: Journal of the Sociology of Self Knowledge, 6*(3), 87–97.

Bransford, J., Brown, A. L., & Cocking, R. R. (Eds.). (2000). *How people learn: Brain, mind, experience, and school.* Washington, DC: National Academy Press.

Burton, R. A. (2008). *On being certain: Believing you are right even when you're not.* New York: St. Martin's Press.

Canadian Council on Learning. (2009, May 4). Homework helps, but not always [Online article]. Retrieved January 1, 2010, from http://www.ccl-cca.ca/CCL/Reports/LessonsInLearning/LinL200900430Homework.htm

Charbit, R., & Kiefer, C. (N.d.). Insight and wisdom: New horizons for leaders [Online article]. Insight Management Partners. Available: http://www.insightmanagementpartners.com/docs/reflections.html

Christensen, C. M., Horn, M. B., & Johnson, C. W. (2008). *Disrupting class: How disruptive innovation will change the way the world learns.* New York: McGraw-Hill.

The Conference Board, The Partnership for 21st Century Skills, Corporate Voices for Working Families, & The Society for Human Resource Management. (2006). *Are they really ready to work? Employers' perspectives on the basic knowledge and applied skills of new entrants to the 21st century U.S. workforce.* Tucson, AZ: The Partnership for 21st Century Skills.

Conley, D. T. (2005). *College knowledge: What it really takes for students to succeed and what we can do to get them ready.* San Francisco: Jossey-Bass.

Costa, A. L. (2008). The thought-filled curriculum. *Educational Leadership, 65*(5), 20–24.

Covey, S. R., Merrill, A. R., & Merrill, R. R. (1994). *First things first: To live, to love, to learn, to leave a legacy.* New York: Simon & Schuster.

Csikszentmihalyi, M. (1990). *Flow: The psychology of optimal experience.* New York: Harper & Row.

Damon, W. (2008). *Path to purpose: Helping our children find their calling in life.* New York: Free Press.

DiChristina, M., Houtz, J., Cameron, J., & Epstein, R. (2008, June/July). Let your creativity soar. *Scientific American Mind,* 24–31.

Dweck, C. S. (2006). *Mindset: The new psychology of success.* New York: Random House.

Epstein, R. (1999). Generativity theory. In M. A. Runco & S. R. Pritzker (Eds.), *Encyclopedia of creativity* (Vol. 1, pp. 759–766). San Diego, CA: Academic Press.

Epstein, R. (2009). Epstein creativity competencies for individuals [Web site]. Retrieved July 8, 2009, from http://mycreativityskills.com

Epstein, R. (2010). Dr. Robert Epstein on creativity and innovation [Video]. Retrieved July 12, 2010, from http://www.youtube.com/watch?v=SR71m0HgdAo

Florida, R. (2004). *The rise of the creative class: And how it's transforming work, leisure, community and everyday life.* New York: Basic Books.

Fried, R. L. (2005). *The game of school: Why we all play, how it hurts kids, and what it will take to change it.* San Francisco: Jossey-Bass.

Fullan, M., Hill, P., & Crévola, C. (2006). *Breakthrough.* Thousand Oaks, CA: Corwin Press.

Gunaratana, B. H. (2002). *Mindfulness in plain English.* Boston: Wisdom Publications.

Guskey, T. R., & Bailey, J. M. (2001). *Developing grading and reporting systems for student learning.* Thousand Oaks, CA: Corwin Press.

Hamilton, J. (2008). Multitasking teens may be muddling their brains [Online article]. NPR.org. Available: http://www.npr.org/templates/story/story.php?storyId=95524385

Hanh, T. N. (1975). *The miracle of mindfulness.* Boston: Beacon Press.

Heinrichs, J. (2009, December). Reverse internships. *Spirit Magazine,* 60–65.

Henderson, J. (2008). Developing students' creative skills for 21st century success. *Education Update, 50*(12), pp. 6–7.

Hoxby, Caroline M. (2003). What has changed and what has not. In P. Peterson (Ed.), *Our schools and our future—Are we still at risk?* (pp. 74–75). Stanford, CA: Hoover Institution Press.

Jensen, E. P. (2008). A fresh look at brain-based education. *Phi Delta Kappan, 89*(6), 408–417. Retrieved January 7, 2009, from http://www.pdkintl.org/kappan/k_v89/k0802jen.htm

Johansson, F. (2004). *The Medici effect: Breakthrough insights at the intersection of ideas, concepts, and cultures.* Boston: Harvard Business School Press.

Johannson, F. (2009, February 22). Volvo's vision for collision safety based on the African grasshopper's vision [Online article]. Retrieved July 12, 2010, from http://www.themedicieffect.com/2009/02

Kaufman, P., Alt, M. N., & Chapman, C. D. (2001). *Dropout rates in the United States: 2000.* Report No. NCES 2002-114. Washington, DC: U.S. Department of Education, National Center for Education Statistics. Available: http://nces.ed.gov/pubs2002/2002114.pdf

Kelley, T. (2001). *The art of innovation: Lessons in creativity from IDEO, America's leading design firm.* New York: Broadway Business.

Labaree, D. F. (2005). Progressivism, schools, and schools of education: An American romance. *Paedagogica Historica, 41*(1 & 2), 275–288.

Lehrer, J. (2009). *How we decide.* Boston: Houghton Mifflin Harcourt.

Marzano, R. J. (2003). *What works in schools: Translating research into action.* Alexandria, VA: ASCD.

Mullis, I. V. S., Martin, M. O., & Foy, P. (2005). *IEA's TIMSS 2003 international report on achievement in the mathematics cognitive domains: Findings from a developmental project.* Chestnut Hill, MA: TIMSS & PIRLS International Study Center, Lynch School of Education, Boston College. Available: http://timss.bc.edu/PDF/t03_download/T03MCOGDRPT.pdf

Multitasking adversely affects brain's learning, UCLA psychologists report [Online article]. Bio-Medicine.org. Available: http://news.bio-medicine.org/medicine-news-3/Multi-tasking-adversely-affects-brains-learning-UCLA-psychologists-report-3771-1/

NAEP Data Explorer [Online database]. (2010). Washington, DC: U.S. Department of Education, National Center for Education Statistics, National Assessment of Educational Progress [Producer].

National Assessment of Educational Progress. (2004a). *The nation's report card: Mathematics highlights 2003.* Washington, DC: National Center for Education Statistics, U.S. Department of Education, Institute of Education Sciences. Available: http://nces.ed.gov/nationsreportcard/pdf/main2003/2004451.pdf

National Assessment of Educational Progress. (2004b). *The nation's report card: Reading highlights 2003.* Washington, DC: National Center for Education Statistics, U.S. Department of Education, Institute of Education Sciences. Available: http://nces.ed.gov/nationsreportcard/pdf/main2003/2004452.pdf

Newport, F. (2009, August 24). Parents rate schools much higher than do Americans overall [Online article]. Retrieved January 2, 2010, from http://www.gallup.com/poll/122432/parents-rate-schools-higher-americans-overall.aspx

O'Connor, K. (2009). *How to grade for learning.* Thousand Oaks, CA: Corwin Press.

Palmer, P. J. (1993). *To know as we are known: Education as a spiritual journey.* San Francisco: HarperSanFrancisco.

Palmer, P. J. (1998). *The courage to teach: Exploring the inner landscape of a teacher's life.* San Francisco: Jossey-Bass.

Partnership for 21st Century Skills. (2008). *21st century skills, education, & competitiveness: A resource and policy guide.* Available: http://www.p21.org/documents/21st_century_skills_education_and_competitiveness_guide.pdf

Partnership for 21st Century Skills. (2009). P21 framework definitions [Online article]. Available: http://www.p21.org/documents/P21_Framework_Definitions.pdf

Peter D. Hart Research Associates. (2005). *Rising to the challenge: Are high school graduates prepared for college and work?* Washington, DC: Author. Available: http://www.achieve.org/files/pollreport_0.pdf

Peter D. Hart Research Associates. (2008). *How should colleges assess and improve student learning? Employers' views on the accountability challenge.* Washington, DC: Author. Available: http://www.aacu.org/leap/documents/2008_Business_Leader_Poll.pdf

Pink, D. (2009). *The surprising science of motivation.* Talk given at TEDGlobal 2009 conference in Oxford, United Kingdom. Available: http://www.ted.com/talks/dan_pink_on_motivation.html

Pink, D. (2005). *A whole new mind: Moving from the information age to the conceptual age.* New York: Riverhead Books.

Prensky, M. (2006). *"Don't bother me Mom, I'm learning."* St. Paul, MN: Paragon House.

Redl, F. (1972). *When we deal with children.* New York: The Free Press.

Report card on America's schools [Online article]. (N.d.). Retrieved December 30, 2009, from http://www.pbs.org/makingschoolswork/hyc/report .html

Ripley, A. (2010, January/February). What makes a great teacher? *Atlantic Monthly*. Retrieved January 17, 2010, from http://www.theatlantic.com /magazine/archive/2010/01/what-makes-a-great-teacher/7841/

Robinson, K. (2006). *Do schools kill creativity?* Talk given at TED2006 conference in Monterey, CA. Available: http://www.ted.com/talks/lang/eng /ken_robinson_says_schools_kill_creativity.html

Rose, L. C., & Gallup, A. M. (2004). The 36th annual Phi Delta Kappa/ Gallup poll of the public's attitudes toward the public schools. *Phi Delta Kappan, 86*(1), 41–56.

Rubin, B. M. (2010, January 20). Teen, tween media use rising. *Chicago Tribune*. Available: http://articles.chicagotribune.com/2010-01-20 /news/1001190509_1_mobile-devices-media-young-people

Rupley, S. (2005). Messaging haze [Online article]. *PCMag.com*. Available: http://www.pcmag.com/article2/0,2817,1823399,00.asp

Ryan, D. (2009, September 25). Meditation can induce long-lasting changes in brain function, scientist says. *Vancouver Sun*.

Sergiovanni, T. J. (2004). Building a community of hope. *Educational Leadership, 61*(8), 33–37.

Svinicki, M., Hagen, A., & Meyer, D. (1996). How research on learning strengthens instruction. In R. J. Menges & M. Weimer (Eds.), *Teaching on solid ground: Using scholarship to improve practice* (pp. 257–288). San Francisco: Jossey-Bass.

Tharp, T. (2003). *The creative habit: Learn it and use it for life*. New York: Simon & Schuster.

U.S. Department of Education, National Center for Education Statistics. (2001, winter). Dropout rates in the United States: 2000 [Online article]. *Education Statistics Quarterly, 3*(4). Retrieved June 22, 2010, from http:// nces.ed.gov/pubs2002/2002607_1.pdf

U.S. Department of Education, National Center for Education Statistics. (n.d.). A summary of findings from PISA 2006 [Online article]. Retrieved June 22, 2010, from http://nces.ed.gov/surveys/pisa/pisa-2006highlights.asp

Wagner, T. (2008). *The global achievement gap: Why even our best schools don't teach the new survival skills our children need—and what we can do about it*. New York: Basic Books.

Wiggins, G., & McTighe, J. (2007). *Schooling by design: Mission, action, and achievement.* Alexandria, VA: ASCD.

Willingham, D. T. (2009). *Why don't students like school?* San Francisco: Jossey-Bass.

Wormeli, R. (2006). *Fair isn't always equal.* Portland, ME: Stenhouse Publishers.

Yazzie-Mintz, E. (2009). *Engaging the voices of students: A report on the 2007 and 2008 high school survey of student engagement.* Bloomington, IN: Center for Evaluation and Education Policy, Indiana University. Retrieved July 13, 2010, from http://indiana.edu/nceep/hssse/images /hssse_2009_report.pdf

Young, R. (N.d.). Lessons learned: All kids can learn [Online article]. Retrieved December 30, 2009, from www.pbs.org/makingschoolswork /ll/all-kids.html

Zmuda, A. (2008). Springing into active learning. *Education Leadership,* 66(3), 38–42.

Zmuda, A., McTighe, J., Wiggins, G., & Brown, J. (2007). *Schooling by design: An ASCD action tool.* Alexandria, VA: ASCD.

Index

The letter *f* following a page number denotes a figure.

About the Author

Allison Zmuda's focus is to help every educator create a competent classroom—a learning environment where all participants believe it is possible for them to be successful—in which what teachers and students are expected to know and be able to do is challenging, feasible, and worthy of the attempt. Zmuda also specializes in short- and long-range continuous improvement planning, evaluating the degree to which structures, policies, and job descriptions support the work of a school to achieve its mission.

Zmuda began her career as a public high school teacher in Connecticut. Her curricular and instructional experiences led her to write her first book, *The Competent Classroom* (2001). Her second book, *High Stakes High School: A Guide for the Perplexed Parents* (2001), welcomes parents into the conversation about standards, assessment, and high-stakes testing. *Transforming Schools: Creating a Culture of Continuous Improvement* (2004), cowritten with Robert Kuklis and Everett Kline, looks at the challenges and promise of engaging in building and systemwide improvement. Zmuda's fourth writing project was as lead co-author of the *ASCD Schooling by Design Action Tool* (2007). Her fifth book, *Librarians as Learning Specialists: Meeting the 21st Century Learning Imperative* (2008), explores the power of libraries as doorways to creating rigor and relevance in student learning.

Zmuda is a faculty member in ASCD's Understanding by Design cadre and also runs her own consulting firm, The Competent Classroom. She has presented at workshops and conferences across the

United States and Canada. In addition, Zmuda hosts "Insider, Outsider," a web-based radio show. She resides in Virginia Beach, Virginia, with her husband and her two children. She can be reached at zmuda@ competentclassroom.com.

Related ASCD Resources

At the time of publication, the following ASCD resources were available; for the most up-to-date information about ASCD resources, go to www.ascd.org. ASCD stock numbers are noted in parentheses.

Books
Activating the Desire to Learn, by Bob Sullo (#107009S25)

Activating and Engaging Habits of Mind, by Arthur L. Costa and Bena Kallick (#100033S25)

The Big Picture: Education Is Everyone's Business, by Dennis Littky and Samantha Grabelle (#104438S25)

The Classroom of Choice: Giving Students What They Need and Getting What You Want, by Jonathan C. Erwin (#104020S25)

Multimedia
Emotional Intelligence Professional Inquiry Kit, by Pam Robbins and Jane Scott (#997146S25)

Project-Based Learning with Multimedia (CD-ROM), by the San Mateo County Office of Education (#502117S25)

Video
High Schools at Work: Creating Student-Centered Learning Three-Tape Series with Facilitator's Guide (#406117S25)

Educating Everybody's Children, Tape 4: Increasing Interest, Motivation, and Engagement (#400225S25)

THE WHOLE CHILD The Whole Child Initiative helps schools and communities create learning environments that allow students to be healthy, safe, engaged, supported, and challenged. To learn more about other books and resources that relate to the whole child, visit www.wholechildeducation.org.

For more information, visit us on the World Wide Web (http://www.ascd.org), send an e-mail message to member@ascd.org, call the ASCD Service Center (1-800-933-ASCD or 703-578-9600, then press 2), send a fax to 703-575-5400, or write to Information Services, ASCD, 1703 N. Beauregard St., Alexandria, VA 22311-1714 USA.